Master Self-Discipline with 7 Powerful Exercises

Daily Blueprint to Cure Procrastination, Laziness, and Develop Habits to Achieve Goals for Entrepreneurs, Weight Loss, and Success in 10 Days

Stephen Mark

© Copyright 2019 - All rights reserved.

The content contained within this book may not be reproduced, duplicated or transmitted without direct written permission from the author or the publisher.

Under no circumstances will any blame or legal responsibility be held against the publisher, or author, for any damages, reparation, or monetary loss due to the information contained within this book. Either directly or indirectly.

Legal Notice

This book is copyright protected. This book is only for personal use. You cannot amend, distribute, sell, use, quote or paraphrase any part, or the content within this book, without the consent of the author or publisher.

Disclaimer Notice

Please note the information contained within this document is for educational and entertainment purposes only. All effort has been executed to present accurate, up to date, and reliable, complete information. No warranties of any kind are declared or implied. Readers acknowledge that the author is not engaging in the rendering of legal, financial, medical or professional advice. The content within this book has been derived from various sources. Please consult a licensed professional before attempting any techniques outlined in this book.

By reading this document, the reader agrees that under no circumstances is the author responsible for any losses, direct or indirect, which are incurred as a result of the use of information contained within this document, including, but not limited to, — errors, omissions, or inaccuracies.

Contents

The Cure to Laziness (This Could Change Your Life) 1

Introduction 2

Chapter 1:
Self-Discipline 7

Chapter 2:
Build Self-Discipline 18

Chapter 3:
The Truth: Self-Discipline Vs Willpower 30

Chapter 4:
Starting Tips for Self-Discipline 42

Chapter 5:
Positive Thinking 55

Chapter 6:
The Secret of Self-Discipline and Entrepreneur 67

Chapter 7:
Secret to Self-Discipline and Addiction, Procrastination and Laziness 77

Chapter 8:
The Secret to Self-Discipline and Weight Loss 93

Chapter 9:
Long-Term Self-Disciplined Habits 106

Chapter 10:
The 3 Proven Methods 117

Chapter 11:
Taking Control of your Life 129

Conclusion 140

Mental Toughness and True Grit 143

Introduction 144

Chapter 1:
Mental Toughness 147

Chapter 2:
Self-Discipline 156

Chapter 3:
Starting Out Tips for Self-Discipline 170

Chapter 4:
Discipline Your Mind like a Navy SEAL 205

Chapter 5:
Become Emotionally Tough 227

Chapter 6:
The 40 Percent Rule 238

Chapter 7:
Positive Thinking 243

Chapter 8:
Long-Term Self-Discipline Habits 246

Chapter 9:
5 Secrets to Building Mental Toughness 266

Chapter 10:
The 7 Rules for Success 271

Chapter 11:
Call to Action 278

The Cure to Laziness (This Could Change Your Life)

Develop Daily Self-Discipline and Highly Effective Long-Term Atomic Habits to Achieve Your Goals for Entrepreneurs, Weight Loss, and Success

Introduction

"My will shall shape my future. Whether I fail or succeed shall be no man's doing but my own. I am the force; I can clear any obstacle before me, or I can be lost in the maze. My choice; my responsibility; win or lose, only I hold the key to my destiny." - Elaine Maxwell

When you take a general look at life, you will discover that it is full of people in various categories of success. Some people tend to enjoy the good things in life. Everything seems to work in their favor, and they live a happy, contented and prosperous life.

Many people start out at a tender age full of potentials, great hopes and aspirations for the future. However, just a few, just a handful of these people can achieve their goal, get a hold of their relationship and succeed in their business and career.

Of the many things that separate the successful class from the unsuccessful ones, self-discipline is a major key. No one plans to fail. As it's often said, success has many children, or should I say family relations. However, how many people are willing to give success what it takes?

We all desire to live the life of our dreams. Marry the girl of our dreams, go for vacation in Hawaii, live a life free from disease of all sorts, be able to buy whatever we need anytime, achieve financial success and be a responsible parent to our kids and a better partner to our spouse. The sad reality, however, is that not everyone is willing to give what it takes to achieve this.

We all know that success doesn't come on a silver platter. Deep down us all, we all know what we must do to make our goals and dream a success, a reality. As an obese person, I know what I must do to lose weight. A student knows what to do to increase the grade and be more successful. A wife/husband knows how they can make their family better and be a better partner for their better half. An addict is very much aware of the steps to break out of the addiction.

Intuitively, we all know what we must do in achieving our goals and making our life better. This is where the problems lie. Are we willing to give what it takes?

For whatever reason, we lack the willpower and discipline to really work towards achieving our goals. Many are less motivated, fond of procrastination, and can't just seem to get the push to strive at whatever it is they set their heart to achieve. Many are fond of making excuses for not getting started. This is where the power of self-discipline comes in.

How beautiful it is to desire to lose weight, set your heart at it and give it all it takes. What a wonderful thing it would be as a student to give it your all to get good grades in college! Committing to that exercise regimen is hard but imagine the wonders it will do to your body and overall health if you could just commit to it!

With the right training and mindset, you can set your heart to achieve anything it wants to achieve. You can train yourself to be strong, develop the right mindset, that of a Navy seal such that when you commit your heart to anything, you become like the wind, clearing away any obstacle standing as a hindrance.

One thing you should know and bear in mind is that people who are successful today are highly disciplined. Besides this, they developed this habit carefully through the mental workout and the right attitude. Imagine a gold medalist in the Olympics for instance. He doesn't just get all good overnight.

Through striving and toiling, through the right power, through discipline and courage, he trains himself. He subjects himself to harsh treatment all in the name of being ahead in the competition. With discipline, he motivates himself, trains himself, and gradually graduates from an amateur to a pro. With time, with self-discipline and resilience as an ingredient, he gradually becomes a professional when the training becomes part of him.

In other words, discipline is a habit that can be learned and developed. You can train it into your life. And if you have picked up this book, you have a very powerful resource in your hand to help you. You are just a step away from achieving whatever it is you set yourself to achieve.

This book will equip and instill in you the practical tool to achieve whatever it is you set your heart to. With the teachings here, you will understand that you can achieve anything. The human mind and will are powerful. With the right motivation and recipe (self-discipline as an ingredient here), it can achieve anything.

Success will no longer be alien to you since your will, coupled with self-discipline, can get you whatever you set your heart on. Then you now realize that successful people, people you count as extraordinary were ordinary men who have mastered the art of self-discipline and habits to achieve their goals.

You are in for a good read my friend. The fact that you chose to read this book rather than go out for a drink with your friends or watch a series on Netflix is an indication that you are just a step away from achieving self-discipline.

Bear in mind that the journey to self-discipline is not an easy one. It is often a lonely road full of temptations and resistance. But one thing

I want you to remember is that you can do it. Set your mind on the goal. Imagine how beautiful and better off your life will be if you persevere and endure to the end. The right attitude and self-discipline, you will be able to surmount all obstacles on your path to realizing your dream.

On a final note, don't be like Jessica who frowns every time her husband drags her away from the bed to go for a jog. Neither be like Tom who feels his parents are punishing him since they seized his Xbox and PlayStation. My point is discipline is not a tool to make your life uncomfortable or necessary unbearable. While I admit that the journey to developing self-discipline is not an easy one, it is worth it. See the journey as a process, a step that will transform you into a better person, a personality you will be proud of.

As you journey through the pages of this book, keep in mind that with self-discipline and the right mindset, you can achieve whatever you set out to!

Chapter 1:
Self-Discipline

"We don't have to be smarter than the rest; we have to be more disciplined than the rest." -Warren Buffett

Self-discipline is one vital skill for success. Additionally, it is so important that the few people that strive to develop this virtue and strengthen it get to reap its benefit in all areas of their life.

Self-discipline simply means the ability to do what is expected of you. It involves doing away with instant gratification or present comfort for the purpose of long-term goals. This explains why Tom's parents had to seize his Xbox to enable him to study hard to get a good grade. Human beings are naturally drawn to entertainment. Hence, Tom's ability to see things from his parents' angle and understand that doing away with present comfort (staying away from Xbox and studying) will be of tremendous benefits for him in the future (good grades).

The fact is, as explained in the introduction, we all know what we need to do to make our life better. However, we lack the self-discipline and zeal to make this happen. It is self-discipline that gives the needed push to overcome the mental and physical barrier to move ahead with what we must do.

In contrary to how many people view self-discipline, it is neither being unreasonably hard/harsh towards yourself nor living a life devoid of fun and interesting things. Rather, self-discipline is one of the indications of inner strength, a form of self-control which enables you to take control of your life, your actions and reactions, and act based on reason and judgment.

Self-discipline gives you the mental toughness to decide and follow through, irrespective of the distractions and inconveniences to deviate. With this, self-discipline is a critical ingredient needed in seeing a goal or vision to reality.

When you have self-discipline, you will be able to stick to your goals and plans and see them through to manifestations. Self-discipline comes in various forms and can be said to be an inner strength giving you the needed boost to kickstart any plan, overcome the initial inertia, stop making excuses, do away with procrastination and follow through what you have got do.

Why Do You Need Self-Discipline?

Take a critical study of successful people in ministry, entertainment, business, and various career fields like celebrities, athletes, footballers, etc. One thing that makes successful ones stand out is the ability to stay focus and extremely disciplined in whatever they set their hearts to.

Hence, while success has many ingredients, self-discipline is like the core ingredient that binds every other part of the recipe. It is a vital habit that can be built over time via conscious and constant effort. It is a habit that many successful people have in common as they have developed and built this into their lives and characters over the years.

I will be sharing personal tips that worked for me, with which I became highly disciplined in life. I am not just sharing some theories or facts here. Rather, inscribed in the pages of this manual are techniques that have been applied to alter my path and take control of my life, career, and relationship for good.

Some years back, I lived a messed-up life and self-discipline was completely alien to me. I carried a lot of aggression and hatred around, especially when I lost my relationship of over five years. A relationship where I devoted my all. The breakup made me very violent and jealous of people with successful relationships. I lost the motivation to do anything tangible in life, and procrastination became the order of the day. I have experienced depression firsthand and never really had anything worthy to live for.

You can imagine how deep I was down the rabbit hole. However, somehow, I managed to get out of this state. This was years back. My transformation was not miraculous, as I took a conscious step to change the course of my life. This was what gave me the motivation to write this book. We as humans learn better through actions, hence, when you read the steps that helped transitioned my life, you will be able to relate. You will live a pretty content life and eventually get the freedom to dictate the course of your life, rather than living life base on impulse.

I have realized that self-discipline is the ability to control your basic desires that stem from pleasure. There are some negative habits that are inherent which many are fond of. Some examples are consuming excess sugar, not going for a workout, hitting the snooze button, avoiding new things, etc. These are negative habits that form the basic desires of man. Hence, an undisciplined man will rather listen to the dictates of his body, take the easy way out and do all the things listed above. However, if you are reading this book, there is a big chance, you are not part of the class described. I believe the desire to pick up this manual and read is the first step in building your self-discipline. You have been able to rise above the limitation and controls of your mind that probably wanted to do other less demanding things. This is one issue of average people who lack self-discipline. They follow the dictate of their mind like a zombie. The willpower and discipline to have a course and stay true to it are absent. This explains why procrastination forms the basis of their life. They are afraid to attempt anything new and they find it easier and preferable to curl up

The Cure to Laziness (This Could Change Your Life)

on the sofa and enjoy a movie rather than take up a task that will build up their mind and life in general.

Humans, generally, at any point in time, is about the body-mind connection. It is the mind that dictates to you. It forces you to do that task another time because you are not feeling like it. It tells you to hit the snooze button for ten more minutes of sleep. When you, however, get a grip on how to put your mind under total subjection, you can confidently say you own your self-discipline!

This explains why one of the major features of self-discipline is the ability to do away with instant gratification and pleasure, in expectation of a future, and much greater gain. This does not come easily, I will admit. Ask many people who have mastered the act of waking up early, I am pretty sure they will affirm that it was not easy at first. Besides, human generally is prone to favor and consider pleasures and things that will not stress them. This is the reason why it is easy to watch a series in one of your home videos, rather than launch your Kindle app and read a book that will make you better off! Self-discipline expresses itself in many ways:

- Perseverance – the ability to keep pushing despite setbacks and obstacles

- Self-Control – the ability to be focused in the face of temptation and distractions

- Resilience – being consistent with a task until you see it through to success

The journey to success is not an easy one. It is laden with distractions, challenges, obstacles, difficulties, and regrets. Yet, if you are going to be successful, you must be willing to rise above these which require self-control, perseverance and persistence, and above all, self-discipline.

When you develop these, you will lead a happy and fulfilled life, with the confidence that you can rise to achieve anything you set your heart to. How awesome is that!

With self-discipline, you get a hold of your life, be in charge and at the driver's seat of your life rather than following the dictates of your mind like a zombie. You live healthily; you accomplish your goals and set yourself up for spiritual improvement and growth.

Self-discipline is very important, and many people are aware of the importance and what you stand to gain from practicing self-discipline. However, only a few are willing to take the steps to develop, train and build their self-discipline. By picking up this book, I bet you are among the few. The pages of this book will equip you with all you need to know.

Benefits and Importance of Self-Discipline

If you were to seek advice from ten successful people, I am pretty sure eight of them will recommend self-discipline at its peak. It is not surprising as self-discipline plays a vital role in the recipe for success. However, what makes self-discipline so important?

- How do you become better off with self-discipline?

- Why is self-discipline vital in every aspect of human life?

Self-Discipline Helps You Feel Healthy

Excessive feeding, junk and fast foods, alcohol, etc. are not good for the health. There are many people out there that are controlled by their impulse to eat and drink. They lack control over their feeding habit when self-discipline is absent. When the inner strength to take charge of their feeding habit is absent, they just cannot seem to control it. Many people are fond of emotional eating – eating when angry, sad, or bored.

With discipline, however, people will stay away from junks, too much pizza, and fat-laden foods. With this, they can save themselves from various diseases that come from excessive sugar.

While many people are completely fine with a cup or two of alcohol, it becomes a problem for others who have turned it into a habit. It is when you are much disciplined that you can resist the urge to open another bottle of alcohol.

A person who drinks excessively hardly shows self-discipline. Therefore, they usually require help in terms of sobriety. And for sobriety to be genuinely effective, a very high degree of self-discipline is vital.

Self-Discipline Helps Form A Habit

Habits are the characters and traits you are known for. Habits are formed with time which can be maintained and solidified via self-discipline. Laziness is a form of habit peculiar to many people. This works against many people's effort to be disciplined.

Being able to wake up as early as 5:00 am is a habit that is already part of many people. This doesn't come naturally; it was developed over time through determination to resist the temptation of hitting the snooze button. And with time, the internal clock of this set of people became aligned with their alarm clock. Hence, once it is 5 am, they wake up.

Self-discipline will make you commit to something, set at it, and give it all it takes to see this to fruition.

Self-Discipline Is Important to Getting Things Done

It is when you have self-discipline that you get to resist procrastination and other distractions. These are the menace that could be vying for your attention at the expense of what you really must do. Self-discipline makes the difference between a student who would read his notebook and the other one who prefers to spend the day with Xbox.

The Cure to Laziness (This Could Change Your Life)

Self-discipline is the basic ingredient you need to set your heart at something and complete it. With this type of character, it gradually becomes your personality, which sets you apart as an achiever in life.

It is the singular habit of self-discipline that makes you a tough personality that never gives up. Since self-discipline has resilience as one of its traits, nothing can stop you hence, you become a rigid and strong personality that is unstoppable.

Self-Discipline Helps You Commit to Exercise and Weight Loss

Many people see physical activities as stress. Yet, medical practitioners made us realize that there are tremendous benefits that come with leading an active lifestyle. Many people will rather curl up on the couch and watch an episode on Netflix, rather than go for a jog. Many will keep telling themselves they will go for that run the coming week, which never happens.

Exercise is however so vital that it can prevent the onset of many diseases in the body. Yet, it doesn't come naturally. It takes self-discipline to pay a gym membership fee and commit yourself to a regular visit. Even if you can't pay for gym membership, going for a walk, an early morning run or jog or any form of exercise all requires discipline.

Exercising your body is vital to your health which helps you lose weight. It is self-discipline that makes you resist distractions and procrastination. With self-discipline comes the inner strength and willpower to decide to exercise your body and commit to it.

Weight loss is not an easy process. It never comes on a platter of gold. It is a step by step process that requires a commitment to something (whether intermittent fasting, constant workout or diet plan) in a bid to get rid of excess fat.

If you want to try to lose weight via intermittent fasting, for instance, you need to religiously schedule you're eating period to a specific window. It takes self-discipline to commit to that. It takes self-discipline to resist the hunger pangs and commit to your endeavor to stay without food for the purpose of losing weight.

If you try to lose weight with a diet plan, it takes self-discipline to commit yourself to follow the meal plan. This involves doing away with junks and many foods that your taste bud finds pleasure in. This cannot happen without self-discipline. This explains why many people don't find success with their diet plan. They commit to it for a week or two and fail.

Self-Discipline Helps You Focus

There are many, many things in this present world that can distract you from your goal. Social media, entertainment, friends, etc., are the common source of distraction that prevents most. With self-discipline, however, you stay faithful and committed to your goal to be successful.

The Cure to Laziness (This Could Change Your Life)

Being focused on your goal ensures you mark off every checklist item that is essential. There are many ingredients crucial for success. Self-discipline is one of the main recipes which also manifest itself as a focus.

To a person that wants to lose weight, for instance, she could have the picture of a model hung up in her bedroom. Every morning, she sees the picture, reminding herself of her goal. This keeps her focused, giving her the motivation to do all she has to do to achieve her goal.

Self-Discipline Brings Out the Best in You

Success never comes on a platter of gold, neither does it goes to the slothful. Every day, if you desire to be successful, you must keep striving to bring out the best in you. An athlete, for instance, needs to practice daily and strive to improve on his previous day performance.

This only happens with self-discipline. It is that ingredient that can keep you on track and help you commit to doing what needs to be done to achieve success.

On the race to success, self-discipline is one of the most important factors that will keep you on track. Without this, there is a high tendency that people with more discipline will knock you out of the race.

Chapter 2:
Build Self-Discipline

Self-discipline is an important ability you must build to gain the best experiences in life. People often feel apprehensive when they hear the term "Discipline" because it is associated with being confined or fixated on a specific routine that makes them feel like they have lost all access to freedom. This popular notion of discipline is far from the truth, and you are about to discover the power that lies within being a self-disciplined individual.

You can't speak about developing willpower and control over your life without first dealing with the concept of discipline. Self-discipline is the capacity you build to control yourself and to make yourself behave in a certain way without needing anybody to tell you what to do. It is also one of the most useful skills you will need in every area of life.

When a person is said to be self-disciplined, it means he/she has gained inner strength and the power to make decisions without being conflicted. This assertion implies that there is a connection between being disciplined and building willpower (We will deliberate more about this in the next chapter). Think about this for a moment, when

The Cure to Laziness (This Could Change Your Life)

was the last time you decided on something and stuck to it till you accomplished it? Do you remember having to create a daily plan and being disciplined enough to see it come to fruition? Have you ever fulfilled an obligation or kept a promise despite stiff oppositions?

If you think back to all the experiences you've had, you will agree that there were times when you wanted to do all you set out to accomplish but fell short of expectations. You didn't fail at such instances, come on, you did well for even trying, but if you had built self-discipline, the chances of succeeding would have been higher.

So, you see, being self-disciplined doesn't mean you get to be so hard on yourself. It merely gives an opportunity to stick to the positive changes, decisions, ideas and action plan you require for a fantastic life. Everyone is at a different level with being self-disciplined, we all have our triumphant moments and our "Keep on trying" moments, but regardless of the level you currently are right now, you should know that the journey to being self-disciplined is a continuous one.

When you decide to be self-disciplined, most of the time, circumstances and situations seem to arise that make it difficult for you to stick to your plan. Now in those moments, it becomes effortless and convenient to let yourself go instead of being guided by discipline.

This situation is a challenge millions of people face all over the world but guess what? There are ways of ensuring that you stick to your plans, read to discover the answers. Self-discipline is not gained when you say, "I want to be a disciplined person", it is also not built when you imitate someone you think is disciplined, neither does it become a reality when you become disciplined for a week after reading this book. Self-discipline can be attained through your habits!

How to Form A Habit?

Habits, yes, those activities you do every day without fail consciously or unconsciously can make or break your journey to be a self-disciplined individual. Your ability to build and sustain the right habits goes a long way in helping you attain the goals and expectations you have for your life.

There are several ways of ensuring you cultivate productive habits, but the most effective step is having a programmed behavioral pattern. The concept of a programmed behavior refers to the way a person builds up his/her resistance level to certain things that hinders the sustainability of a good habit. Experts on this subject suggest that if your habits prevent you from being self-disciplined, you must develop new ones, but there is a caveat.

Developing new patterns is not the problem, breaking away from the old ones is where the challenge lies and until you handle this issue, you will never attain the level of self-discipline you desire.

So, we are back to the most viable solution you can implement which entails developing a programmed behavior. Here's a scenario, you know the importance of reading, as such you resolve to read more

The Cure to Laziness (This Could Change Your Life)

books this year. For you to accomplish this goal, it is essential that you stop attending parties on weeknights. Now, this friend of yours invites you over for a party just as you are about to start reading a book; suddenly you feel tempted to attend one last party after all, one party wouldn't hurt.

You put your shoes on, have a great time at the event but it will be harder for you to say "No" the next time you are invited. Gradually, you forget about the commitment you made to reading and go back to the partying habits which contribute to a lack of self-discipline in your life.

However, if you had a programmed behavior, you will be able to resist the temptations and stick to your new habits, so what is it exactly? A programmed behavior means being intentional with your habits; it is a manner of conducting yourself in such a way that you are 100% committed to your new traditions.

There are two phases to building a programmed behavior; the first stage requires the individual getting rid of the bad habit and the second stage entails replacing that bad habit with a good pattern.

Once you get both phases set up, you must ensure that you stick to them regardless of the enticement. A person who has adopted a programmed behavior will decline the invitation to a party and immediately start reading, shutting out every other consideration that will lead to a change of plans. This is how you build self-discipline with your habits; by being deliberate with the decisions you take.

It takes a while to form a new habit, but you can get ahead of time by starting and repeating the new habit daily until you succeed. The first few days of implementation might seem like a daunting challenge, but if you persist, you will become more comfortable with time.

When you think about a programmed character, cast your mind back to an automated machine; such a device will only render products and services it is programmed to give. The same applies to you; a programmed mindset can only allow what the new habits entail so not giving in to the wrong habits become natural to you.

Programmed behavior also helps you remain constantly reminded of your goals; you become fixated on what you want to accomplish that you don't give room for anything less. This approach to self-discipline works with any goal you set for yourself: weight loss, career goals, etc. First, program your mind to resist wrong and stick to good then you will be on your way to becoming a self-disciplined person.

Exercise is an activity that can help you build a programmed behavior. If you are a fitness enthusiast, you will agree that the process of keeping fit is one that demands some programming of the mind. Fitness practices must be done according to the dictates of time and effort; to achieve certain milestones, you must be doing or must have done some severe activities.

The Cure to Laziness (This Could Change Your Life)

If you want to become a very self-disciplined person using the principle of programmed behavior, you may have to start taking exercises seriously. The connection between exercises, habits and self-disciplined lies in the fact that with exercises there are a lot of routines, sets and timings one must rely on. A person struggling with sustaining a new habit will find it easier to do so if he/she starts taking exercise seriously.

So, the same determination used to attain a 10,000-step walk can be used to say "No" when necessary and stick to the newly formed habit. Exercise is also a positive habit that leads to the development of other outstanding traditions such as resting, drinking more water, and engaging in healthier activities that inspire you to maintain good habits.

As you create and maintain an exercise schedule, you will also be doing the same with your new patterns, and this is all because you decided to have a programmed behavior towards life. As you work on implementing a programmed behavior, you shouldn't miss out on building a new personality. Old habits have a way of affecting our characters; you do something for so long until it becomes a part of you.

So, try positive things today, set the old ways aside by being committed to a sustainable process which guarantees self-discipline. Discipline is all about control; it is about your ability to take charge of your life and determine what is right for you while sticking to it. Why will anyone want to exercise control? Why can't we live the way we want to? Why are you reading this book learning about how to be self-disciplined? There are so many "Why's" to answer, and until you provide answers, you will not get the best out of this experience.

Determine Your Why

Getting to know the reason for attaining self-discipline will give you an encouraging boost that will cause you to be more focused on your long-term goals as opposed to being concerned about immediate fulfillment. You can know why you are doing this through goals; your goals must be powerful enough to set you sailing on the right course and help you resist the temptation of going back to bad habits that stifle you.

A lot of times when individuals set goals, they try to attain the goals and hope that the process will help them become better with being disciplined. However, when they observe that they are still not as disciplined as they want to be, they become frustrated with the effort and quickly give up. The problem isn't with goal setting; it is with the quality of goals you set. You must have explicit goals; this refers to targets that are detailed enough to provoke an essential response from you. Shall we relate to the scenario used when discussing habits?

Setting a goal to read more books in a year isn't powerful enough as such when your friend sends an invitation for a party on a weeknight, you will oblige because you didn't give your goals enough details. On the other hand, if you had explicitly mentioned that your aspiration to read two books per month and a total of 24 books in a year, you will have created a compelling goal.

Now, having this exact intention in mind will cause you to decline the invitation because at that time, you are probably still on one book and it is already the second week of the month. When you have a specific goal, it causes you to think about the long-term result that goal will fetch you and all these considerations will make it possible for you to stay focused on attaining the vision thus fighting off the temptation that makes you undisciplined. Simply put, make your goals come alive with facts!

The next step you should take after setting goals is to utilize the power of imagination. Now that you are armed with the right aspirations, it is crucial that you start thinking about the results even now.

What do you want to achieve with these goals? How will you feel when you eventually smash the objectives and win? Time spent thinking about the possible outcomes of your goals is instrumental in helping you stay motivated enough to accomplish your set targets. So, there you are, visualizing how you will be after hitting your target of 24 books in a year, think of how much knowledge you will acquire that will be contributory in helping you grow career-wise.

Envisaging your goal is a good step but there is something even better than that, and it is being focused on the progression you make towards the goal. If you have taken the time to create a goal that helps you read two books every month, you should be concerned about how you are going to achieve this.

To become a self-disciplined person, you must be committed to the realization of the process as much as you are committed to fulfilling the goal. People are always so fixated on the goal, wanting to attain a certain height but they forget that there is a process to follow as such if the process isn't right, the target will not be achieved.

You've got to train your mind to create a method that will be effective in attaining your goals. Using the situation, we've been working with, this means that you must be willing to create a "Reading plan" that suits your schedule and enables you to read the set number of books in that month. If you stay focused on this process long enough, if you are consumed with the idea of doing it, you will achieve your long-term goals.

Now that you can create the right habits and be more specific with your goals, you are closer to establishing the pathway to being self-disciplined. If you are wondering if there is still one more stop to make, you are right, we must talk about the concept of being absorbed with original ideas.

Focus on Essential Tasks

The Cure to Laziness (This Could Change Your Life)

Being self-disciplined is not about being frustrated and forced to do the things you don't like just because you want to attain specific goals. On the contrary, it is possible to be a disciplined person who still loves whatever he/she does. If you are going to develop and build up a new habit, it should be something you do because you will enjoy it as opposed to doing it because everyone else requires it of you.

This means that if you must engage in exercises for the sake of your health and someone suggests walking around the neighborhood, you can decline if that form of exercise isn't fun for you. You can try swimming, jogging, weightlifting or something else that will help you exercise and still achieve your goals; this is how you concentrate on the basic ideas.

In a bid to do it all, some people end up feeling flustered, unhappy and depressed about not being self-disciplined. The problem can be traced to the fact that they are doing all these activities to impress others and until they start to focus on fundamentals, they will continue to struggle.

This is a vital lesson you must instill: don't try to accomplish so many tasks at once. Yes, you've got the passion for doing more, and you are ready to take up the challenge, but would it be better if you tried to do these numerous things and felt overwhelmed or would you prefer to do what you genuinely enjoy?

If your affirmative answer is to the latter question, then you must set goals and form new habits that fit into the plan you've got for your life. Take on the reading challenge because you love books, not because you feel compelled to do it.

As you redirect your energies towards things that excite you, there will be a significant change with the level of discipline you enjoy, and this will also help you have a firmer grip on your goals.

To summarize the notion of being absorbed with basic ideas, you should do what you love and not what you are expected to do. Enjoy the tasks that are best suited for your life and bask in the feel of being able to live freely. If you are going to be self-disciplined, you shouldn't engage in tasks you find unnecessary; redirect your energies to things you can do joyfully while maintaining your stance.

Mostly, you should do the things you believe will work for you; the importance of this aspect cannot be overemphasized because there are too many people who misunderstand the message of discipline. Such persons become so stiff with life, living every day doing what they think they "Should" do as opposed to doing what they "Love" to do. For a fact, you will become more disciplined when you are living on your own terms because you are not pressured by any task or forced to do something you are not comfortable with.

By being selective with what you choose to do, you empower yourself to live by your own rules which is instrumental in increasing your

The Cure to Laziness (This Could Change Your Life)

level of discipline. Taking on more than what you can handle is a sign of being undisciplined and the only way to rectify this is by sticking to the principle of selectivity. Be careful with what you decide to take on; all your decisions, habits and goals should be motivated by what you enjoy.

The journey to becoming a self-disciplined person is an enduring one, but you have taken the first step which is quite commendable. You must continue to mold yourself daily with real concepts and action plans that give you the desired results. In the next chapter we continue our discourse on self-discipline from a refreshing perspective, do enjoy the read.

Chapter 3:
The Truth: Self-Discipline Vs Willpower

"Willpower is what separates us from the animals. It's the capacity to restrain our impulses, resist temptation – do what's right and good for us in the long run, not what we want to do right now. It's central, in fact, to civilization." -Dr. Roy Baumeister, Ph.D.

If you want to achieve anything significant in life you must be self-disciplined; this is a fundamental truth to embrace first before anything else. When a person starts to feel like he/she has achieved less of the kind of success that was anticipated, the problem can be traced to the absence of discipline.

There is also the concept of willpower which is gaining a lot of attention these days with people who want to do better with their lives. But before we consider the idea behind willpower, you should know why it is an alternative tool for self-discipline.

When people struggle with any form of addiction or personal issue, they tend to try and muscle their way out of it by showing the power

The Cure to Laziness (This Could Change Your Life)

of their "Will" against that problem. But think about it this way, will there be a problem in the first place if they were disciplined?

Self-discipline Vs. Willpower underscores the importance of taking care of a potential problem even before it becomes an actual challenge. With the former idea, you are taking charge, not giving room for an issue.

While with the latter, you are trying to take on a full battle with the problem hoping that as you go "cold turkey" on it, there will be a difference. When you understand the differences between both ideals, you will become empowered to use them right.

There is a time when willpower becomes useful in life generally, but it can't be used to replace the importance of self-discipline. In this chapter, you are going to discover some striking similarities between self-discipline and willpower.

You will also become conversant with the reason why self-discipline trumps the idea of willpower when dealing with life's issues. Willpower has its advantages, but the major point is that it shouldn't be used as a substitute for self-discipline. So, what is willpower?

Willpower refers to the unwavering strength to perform one's wishes; it is also the ability to control one's impulses or actions. Considering willpower from the perspective of dealing with an issue, it is a concept that teaches you to use all your mental, emotional and physical strength to deal with the problem and win.

If you have been dealing with an addiction or exposure to bad habits with willpower, you will try to fight it off. When you eventually win, you will feel good for a moment, but you might become vulnerable to a relapse.

With self-discipline, you train your mind, body, and soul to resist the issues you are dealing with, and this training is what helps you establish stability and consistent growth such that your success story becomes a source of encouragement to other people.

Self-Discipline: A Training Channel

When self-discipline is viewed as a training process, it starts to work for an individual. Do you remember when you were in school? How you needed the help of your tutor to understand some of the most complex topics taught?

Well, that tutor made it possible for you to develop a study pattern which became part of the reasons why you became successful in school. Every tutor sets the foundational idea on which the student's academic success is built upon.

However, your tutor couldn't have been with you all the time, he/she wouldn't write the examination for you as well so what do you do?

The Cure to Laziness (This Could Change Your Life)

Firstly, you must understand that the tutor's role is consultative, a more significant percentage of the work to be done lies within you.

This is often the problem with people who struggle with self-discipline; they want the tutor with them all the time, they are not willing to do things on their own. A dietician must remind them to eat the right foods, a gym instructor must push them to exercise, and when these "Tutors" are not available, they fall like a pack of cards.

Self-discipline is a training channel that offers you a unique opportunity to do the things that are right by you without anyone compelling you to. When you start to imbibe the principles of being disciplined, you train yourself to identify the areas you should focus on while working towards being self-reliant (we will discuss on the concept of being self-reliant very soon).

You might need a tutor at the beginning of your journey (everyone needs a helping hand) but after the tutor gives you the necessary training, get on with the processes and protocols on your own. Train yourself daily to carry out those activities your tutor has taught you and gain mastery over them. Self-discipline doesn't mean you must deprive yourself of some things; it just says that you are willing to train yourself until you attain a level of expertise.

When you realize that you are training yourself for the future, you put your goals in focus and strive to attain them. So, at this point, you are not propelled by the desire to impress your tutor; instead, you are inspired by the image of success and fulfillment you visualize upon achieving your objectives.

The result of being self-disciplined is independence. You know you are closer to the goal of being self-disciplined when you start to do those positive things that transform your life for good.

Being Self-Reliant

While the training process to becoming self-disciplined doesn't end, it does contribute to making you an independent person. So back to the tutor story, as you listen and imbibe all the tutor teaches, you start to understand why being self-disciplined is essential.

Gradually, you begin to do those things that uplift you without seeking the guidance of your tutor. Now what happens to you is that you start to trust yourself again, you say to yourself "I can do this," and you watch those things come to life.

Being self-reliant is an aspect of self-discipline some people never attain because they don't have enough faith in themselves. They take one step out of that addiction problem today and take several steps backward. They try to drink more water for a week and become dehydrated for another month.

Until there is a commitment to your progress, you will struggle with being over-reliant on your tutor. You've got to understand that while a tutor is a guide, you are the executor. No one will ever understand

The Cure to Laziness (This Could Change Your Life)

your desire to be better at what you do better than you, which is the reason why it is your responsibility to push yourself despite having a tutor.

You might want to ask, "How do I know when I become self-reliant?" Well, you will know that you have become independent when you carry out the activities that propel you to make progress WITHOUT anyone's nudging.

This means you wake up in the morning for that early run around the park if you have a fitness challenge. The wrong foods are thrown out of the refrigerator if you are dealing with a weight problem. You get to read more books if you want to attain more knowledge and you do all that is required of you on your own terms. When you start to do these things, you can tell that you are now a self-reliant person who can make progress without being told what to do.

Another way you can tell if you are becoming independent is when you find yourself motivating other people to attain their goals as well. They say the best way to become more is by giving more and you cannot inspire someone else if you still struggle with your reality.

The moment you start acting like a tutor to someone else who struggles with a similar challenge just like you, that is the moment when you have become the best version of yourself.

Self-discipline empowers you thus creating multiple avenues through which you can help someone else become better. You start to see yourself as a tutor as well. Being able to help someone else will solidify all you know and set you on the course to consistent success with whatever you are dealing with.

The fact that you become self-reliant doesn't mean you also become a perfectionist with discipline. There will be challenging times when it seems like you are not so confident. What can you do when faced with such a trial?

Failure Is Part of The Process

The fact that you recognize how powerful it is to be self-disciplined is commendable, but beyond that, you should prepare for the eventuality of making mistakes and learning from them. People get into trouble for relying on willpower alone. If you are going to focus on willpower as an alternative to self-discipline, you will not be able to handle mistakes when they happen. This is because willpower makes you believe that you can do it all.

With willpower there is no preparation for failure at any time during the process, so with you not being prepared for failure, you might give in to the problem when mistakes occur. Self-discipline prepares you for success and empowers you with the right mindset to handle errors. As it is with other training opportunities, you will become conversant with the steps you can take when there is an unexpected challenge.

So, being self-disciplined or having willpower doesn't exempt you from problems but self-discipline makes you develop a tough skin such that you can deal with those mistakes if they happen.

You may have had a plan to change your diet because you want to look trim and fit. Even after sticking to healthy meals for a while, you might experience a "Fall" someday which makes you eat potato chips forgetting that you are on a strict diet.

If you were focused on willpower, you would be devastated, thinking "What have I done?" "I thought I was strong enough to handle this," but if you were relying on the training you've got with discipline, you would realize that "Yes, I made a mistake, but I am not going back to it, neither will I let this error get the best of me."

Self-discipline doesn't make you feel less of yourself when you make a mistake; it's all a part of the training process. It's like being in school, you pass some tests excellently, and then you don't excel with others, but you keep pressing on knowing that both the good and the not so good ones contribute to giving you a fantastic experience.

Failure as a part of the process shouldn't give you the leeway to make mistakes intentionally. But it helps you become comfortable with the idea of failing that you are not frightened by it.

In the absence of the fear of failure, you will be confident enough to face your future with positive expectations. Once you deal with the challenge of fear, you can achieve a lot on this journey to self-discipline.

Learning Never Ends

One of the most fantastic feelings you enjoy when you are a self-disciplined individual is that you get to learn every day! Yes, there is a lesson for you to gain daily and it all contributes to making the process of being disciplined even easier.

As opposed to be a person who uses willpower and continually wants to rely on the ability of self, self-discipline allows you to learn from everything. You get to learn from your environment, the decisions you make and every other experience you create on this journey.

If you are self-disciplined, you will be self-conscious as well. There is an awareness you have that makes it possible for you to take note of everything you do. This means you get to learn more about what is right and what isn't right for you thus helping you make better choices.

If you are thinking about kicking out your addictions, you will have to be self-disciplined first; not just because you want to fight off the addiction but because you are willing to learn more about yourself.

The Cure to Laziness (This Could Change Your Life)

Some therapists who try to help people out with challenges discover that when a person is self-disciplined, he/she tends to find new ways of tackling the problem on their own because we are programmed to learn lessons about ourselves when we are disciplined.

Think about this; the moments you lived without being conscious of discipline were probably the times when you felt like you couldn't handle the challenges you were faced with. This was also because you weren't aware of yourself nor your potentials.

Self-discipline makes it possible for you to always keep your life in perspective and this is a significant pathway to continuous learning. You become aware of your strengths and weaknesses while enjoying the former and working on the latter.

If you are currently struggling with something you want to change in your life; a habit, thought process or issue, focus on being self-disciplined and you will be able to solve the problems without getting help from a third party.

The principle of continuous learning by being self-disciplined helps an individual take responsibility for their actions. It is easy to blame someone else for our errors when we aren't disciplined enough to see where we falter.

If you have ever disciplined a child before, you probably heard all sorts of excuses from the child "It wasn't my fault" "It was Dilly who tipped the cup over, I just watched it trip and spill."

As funny as these simple childish responses are, you get to see that the undisciplined child never takes responsibility and it is the same for adults. If you are going to be the best version of yourself by being disciplined, while learning consistently with a strength of character, you must be willing to take responsibility for your actions.

Remember that you are on a journey; you may wobble off the track at some point, but you can always return to the records and keep up. This is another reason why self-discipline is better than willpower.

The desire to become achievers is innate in everyone, from the time individuals start to learn about life till the day they die, there will always be a consistent quest for attainment, but only one thing is needful to make it happen; self-discipline.

This chapter has been all about juxtaposing two compelling concepts in a bid to show which one works best and how you can utilize it for your long-term plans. If you have been struggling with challenges, habits, and addictions, it is probably because you are using willpower.

Build up your character and increase your capacity to always do the right things by being self-disciplined. Think about being disciplined as the foundational ideal you must implement first before considering

The Cure to Laziness (This Could Change Your Life)

willpower. You will be motivated to put up a fight with whatever you want to change (willpower) after you have toughened yourself up with training that helps instill a sense of discipline in you.

You are still on this journey to being self-disciplined; there are so many instructions and ideas to grasp from other sections. While you anticipate the content of the chapters to come, get ready to gain access to useful starting tips that will help you overcome challenges with self-discipline every day.

Chapter 4:
Starting Tips for Self-Discipline

"It is our choices that show what we truly are, far more than our abilities." -J.K. Rowling

You now have an advanced understanding of what self-discipline is about, from basic concepts to comparisons to other similar ideas that form the foundational beliefs of the subject matter.

We have succeeded in creating a pattern of information that aids the process of self-discipline for you. It is essential that you always remind yourself of all you've discovered thus far because the ideas are in a sequence.

This chapter takes things up a notch by introducing some of the most useful tips you can imbibe before becoming a disciplined individual. When you get to the end of this chapter, you will start taking proactive measures towards bringing these tips to life through actionable plans.

The Cure to Laziness (This Could Change Your Life)

The previous chapter espoused on the relationship between self-discipline and willpower, and facts which explained why you should be focused on developing the former.

However, in that detailed chapter, you weren't shown the tips to implement that will help you choose discipline over willpower, so the objective of this chapter is to teach you all about that and more.

You should note that these tips will be most effective when you stick to them for an extended period. The best way to achieve sustainable results is by incorporating solutions to daily routines.

The previous chapter elaborated on the idea of self-discipline being a training process; now you should hold that thought in mind as you read through because what you will discover in this chapter are the tools needed for the training.

Remove Temptations

Everyone who is trying to become better with self-discipline is trying to get over some challenge or personal problem that causes them a lot of discomforts. It might be dealing with procrastination, addictions, weight gain, lack of focus, or whatever troubles your mind.

The problem will not just go away because you want it to, neither is it going to dissipate because you suddenly realize the importance of self-discipline. You need to know that every issue a human being is faced with is triggered by certain factors.

If you discover that you always go to work late despite having good intentions, don't try to wake up and go to work early the following day, you need first to discover why you have been going to work late all the time; this is how you take care of a problem from its roots.

When you get the reasons, you become aware of your temptations, and you've got to remove them immediately. Eliminating temptation means getting rid of the things that serve as distractions to you.

Whatever you do that makes you go back to the same habits or patterns that are not productive is a distraction, and until you figure out how to get rid of them for good, you will consistently struggle with the problem. So, you know what you are dealing with; it might even be something worse than being late to work, it might be a challenge no one knows you are dealing with. Well for you to cross over to the self-disciplined side, you need to detoxify your life.

Your desire to become a self-disciplined person will never be attained if you keep going back to feed what tempts you, even when you do it in secret. The temptation must go, and it does take an amount of discipline to do that.

If you want to be more productive at work, you must show up early enough to get started with the day's activities. Going to bed late the previous night is an example of temptation with the ripple effect. So, what do you do?

The Cure to Laziness (This Could Change Your Life)

You must set up restrictive measures that make it possible for you to go to bed early so you can wake up on time the following day. One of such restrictive rules includes having dinner on time, turning off the tv before bedtime, and sleeping at a designated time every evening.

The fact that you set such restrictive measures doesn't mean the temptation goes away immediately. Your body will try to resist, but if you persist, you will get used to it. Addiction can also be very challenging especially when it's a secret, but you can get over that addiction and live freely. First, discover the temptations and cut them off.

As you set up those restrictive barriers, get an accountability partner who checks up on you and monitors your progress. An accountability partner can be a close friend who is very disciplined, your boss at the office (if it is a work-related challenge) or a third-party expert who can help you get back on track when you miss a step.

To become a self-disciplined person, you must be selective with everything you do; some activities will set you back, and others will inspire you to become better. Eliminate the distractions and temptations while focusing on definite ideas that bring you closer to the goal.

Watch What You Do

As you disregard the temptations and distractions, also remember to become conscious of when you feel hungry, angry, tired or lonely.

These are feelings that make you vulnerable and cause you to be undisciplined.

So, you need to understand why you feel the way you do and then figure out a way to get out of it immediately. Watching what you do refers to being conscious of how your feelings drive you to action.

If you are trying to become healthier through the foods you eat, your body might not warm up to the fruits and veggies you feed it, so you are bound to feel "Hungry" at some point.

Now feeling hungry here means the desire for the kind of unhealthy foods you used to enjoy. Instead of you getting the potato chips, burgers and lots of carbs, try to decipher why you feel hungry and then eat more of the healthy stuff because that is what self-disciplined people do.

If you have had a sad upbringing with lots of family issues, you are bound to feel angry every day. Your anger wouldn't steam from what happens around you but comes from within you.

You should figure out what makes you angry and deal with it! Even if it is an event from the past, be courageous, forgive those who hurt you and move on in faith. You are on the road to becoming a self-disciplined individual, and this means you must become bold about reaching out to what makes you an even better person. If you are angry, try to be calm.

The Cure to Laziness (This Could Change Your Life)

When a person is tired, he/she will most likely not make good decisions and this why when you feel tired - get some rest. It is okay to take a break from everything else that competes for your attention and relax.

For you to be self-disciplined, you should know when your body and mind needs to get detached. But if you continue to push yourself, you will start to feel agitated which gives room for you to make wrong decisions.

Are you dealing with the loss of a loved one? Have your friends deserted you or are you surrounded by a lot of people but still feel lonely? You cannot make progress with self-discipline feeling this way.

Loneliness makes a person feel like he/she doesn't have to be accountable to anyone else, so that gives room for bad decisions. Whenever you feel lonely, reach out to someone, if you are overwhelmed by trouble, get friends and family to help.

You are not an island, and everyone needs help at some point in their lives. Being self-disciplined means, you love who you are enough to make the right decisions for yourself, and if you fancy yourself, you will reach out to those who can help when you need it the most.

Always watch what you do; your actions are a product of your feelings so check on yourself often. How are you feeling now? Why do you think that way? What can be done to make it all better? Get answers and don't stay too vulnerable for long.

Don't wait for it to "Feel right."

Waiting for the feeling is like waiting for the good decisions you make to "Feel right," and if you continue to wait, you will be passing on a brilliant opportunity to become self-disciplined.

Now we need to get into the human brain for a few moments here; there are two parts of the brain, one aids your habits and the other your decisions. The role of your brain that focuses on decisions loves to stick to a routine.

That part of your brain is used to the predictable decisions you will take so there is often no room for changes or new choices. Now if you want to get better with being self-disciplined, you must make changes with everything that pertains to your life.

This means that when you do go ahead to make the changes, your brain tries to reject it, and this makes you feel uncomfortable. At this stage, you start to "Feel" like maybe you shouldn't implement the changes anymore, but you cannot afford to do so!

You shouldn't wait for the perfect sunny feeling that gives you an affirmative nudge, and whenever you feel like you shouldn't be doing something new, that is the right time to do it.

The Cure to Laziness (This Could Change Your Life)

That feeling of being uncomfortable is what strengthens the new habit you are about to form. Your mind or your brain may not be prepared for the change, but for you to be self-disciplined, you need to shut down that feeling and stick to what you know is required.

If you have been struggling with a problem, a bad habit or an addiction, it is probably because your mind is trying to reject the new ideas you want to implement.

If you were born and raised in a city and lived there for a long time as an adult, you will find that you have become accustomed to the food, their way of life and tiny details that make the place home.

When you move away for a while even for a short vacation, you will not get used to the food and lifestyle of the new place overnight. The food might taste too spicy, the environment might feel cold and you start to feel like you should go home.

If you hold on for a few more days, you will get used to the new environment, but if you give up and go home, you will probably never get used to anywhere else, and that's just sad.

Your journey to being self-discipline is like the experience you have in a new place, if you wait until it all feels perfect, you will lose out on the experience entirely. For self-discipline to be possible, you must look beyond your feelings, else you will be ruled by them.

Schedule Breaks

While trying to be self-disciplined, it is possible to get carried away with the process and forget to take a break. You've come a long way, even with this book and you deserve a treat.

However, in a bid to give yourself a treat, you shouldn't go back to the habits you are trying to abstain from. Before you give yourself one, make sure you have done something worthy, like a milestone.

Planning breaks make it possible for you to appreciate how far you have come while anticipating more success. The idea behind self-discipline can be taken so seriously by some people that they are not willing to do anything else except being disciplined.

When you go a long way and do good to yourself by reaching your goals, take a breather and chill off the pressure. You are not supposed to be immensely consumed with the idea of being disciplined, else you will feel stressed.

So, what is that thing you've always wanted to buy for yourself? How about dinner at an excellent restaurant? You could go to the park and have a nice time with your kids (if you have any), ice cream, etc.

Taking a break helps you get an honest assessment of how far you have come with being disciplined and what more you can do to get better. But in that state of relaxation, your mind is also at peace, and you feel like you have broken even with the process.

The Cure to Laziness (This Could Change Your Life)

If you have been trying to get over an addiction for a while, set a target for yourself entailing what you should do on a daily, weekly, monthly and yearly basis. When you hit your daily goal, give yourself a high-five or a pat on the back.

If you hit your weekly goals, oh that calls for some ice cream and a sweet little treat. With your monthly successes, you can get yourself a nice present and when you hit the significant annual milestone, do something nice for yourself (something you have never done before).

The rewards and treats will also serve as an encouraging factor for you on this journey to self-discipline. Thinking about what you will do for yourself when you reach a milestone will propel you always to do your best.

It's like a child who waits for the treats from Santa Claus every Christmas, the child becomes well-behaved to be on Santa's good books, and that is how this process will be for you.

Be intentional about taking breaks periodically, in fact; you should work towards the breaks such that when you are ready to celebrate, you have the right resources. More importantly, it takes a lot of discipline to hit a target so in a bid to reach that goal you set for yourself, you will take disciplined steps that take you closer to your goal. You will fight off the addiction, kick off that bad habit and recreate a new life for yourself.

Forgive Yourself

As mentioned in a previous chapter, becoming self-disciplined is a process that isn't entirely smooth. You will be putting your best foot forward but will be faced with stiff opposition especially if you have practiced that bad habit or addiction for a long time.

Regardless of how many times you experience a relapse, you must be willing to forgive yourself and move on. Yes, there are going to be some slip-offs, and you will feel disappointed in yourself especially if you had faith in your ability to handle the situation.

However, forgiveness should come naturally to you. Being hard on yourself for making mistakes isn't the right move. When you are open about your vulnerability, you become empowered to minimize errors.

So, assuming the errors do happen, what you should do is share your failings with someone you trust. If you have an accountability partner, he/she will be the best person to share your feelings with.

After sharing, forgive your errors and make a promise to yourself that you wouldn't fall short of expectations again. Now that you are on the pathway to self-discipline, it will inspire you to fulfill your promises and keep your word.

This tip is one of the reasons why you were admonished not to depend on willpower earlier. With willpower, you will want to lean on your ability and physical strength forgetting that these factors can be affected.

Don't rely on willpower, just be disciplined enough to acknowledge when you are wrong and live freely. Shame has a cruel way of taking over your freedom; it makes you feel like you haven't achieved anything so it shouldn't be encouraged.

First, be committed to the process, do your best, don't compromise on the standards and let the process be your focal point. When you do all these, you have ticked the relevant boxes, but did you know that people still failed in their attempt to become self-disciplined even after trying these?

So, doing everything by the books isn't a guarantee that you wouldn't experience some failings on your part. Just continue to do the right things, pick yourself up when you fall and keep your eyes on the goal.

You have a responsibility to encourage yourself every day; if you make a mistake, you can tell yourself, "Oh that was a bad day, but I will do better next time" these real push-ups make it possible for you to stay on course.

Don't hold a grudge against yourself and don't be angry at your shortcomings. Sometimes these errors in judgment help strengthen your resolve to become the most self-disciplined person who can hold his/her head high and still make a lot of personal impacts.

We are always listening to messages and reading books that urge us to forgive others who err while showing kindness to people who make mistakes. But what about you? Who forgives you when you aren't at your best? So be kind to yourself as well; be patient with your process and have some faith in yourself.

While striving to become a self-disciplined person, learn to show some compassion to yourself. There will be days when you don't feel so confident but even on those days, continue to do your best.

Tips for self-discipline are motivating factors that can inspire you daily. It can be a fascinating time for you if you want to lose weight and get a "Bikini body," but it also means that you must put in the work to make it happen.

Before you start visualizing the hot body making a beach debut, you must put in the work, and by "Work" we mean being self-disciplined. The ideas shared in this chapter will not only get you the beach body (or any other thing you want), they will also help you glean a life-long lesson that affects every other area of your life.

Positive thinking plays a very crucial role in helping you develop self-discipline; you will be amazed at the kind of progress you make with this journey when your mind is tailored to think only positive thoughts.

Chapter 5:
Positive Thinking

"Define success on your own terms, achieve it by your own rules, and build a life you're proud to live." -Anne Sweeney

There is a connection between the thought process and discipline, the way a person thinks consistently will affect the kind of progress he/she makes with being self-disciplined. In this chapter, you are going to learn about the crucial role positive thinking plays in helping you become better with discipline.

Every minute you spend thinking about something, you invest in your personality, this investment process works without you knowing it, but over time, you start to manifest the traits of the thoughts you encourage in your mind.

There are two kinds of thought processes; the positive and the negative. Whatever mindset makes you feel good, inspired and encouraged to become a better version of yourself is often birthed through positive thoughts. Of course, the defeatist mentality which makes you think you are undeserving, and incapable is a product of negative thinking.

Anyone presented with both thinking patterns will choose positivity, but it doesn't work that way. You don't get to "Choose" what you want to think about; it isn't something you pick up and use.

Positive thinking is a concept that is adopted and continuously refined through time. Although some people doubt its efficacy, it doesn't undermine the fact that when utilized, you can make a lot of progress with whatever you want to achieve.

You are reading this book because of the keyword "Self-discipline" yet if you can establish a routine that encourages you to think positively, you will get the same results in every other area of your life as well.

Thoughts and Personality

The mind is a force field, it is the most powerful tool humans possess; from within it, thoughts proceed, and these thoughts stir up emotions that affect the quality of life a person lives.

The emotions that come from the mind serve as materials for the formation of words, the words you speak to yourself and others portray your personality. So, if a person exposes his/her mind to negative thoughts, the resulting emotions will be adverse as well which also means that the person's words would be uninspiring even to self.

The Cure to Laziness (This Could Change Your Life)

As this individual try to build self-discipline, there will be trials, because there was no prior training in positive thinking, the person is unable to handle the problems.

At this point, negative words start to pop out "I can't do it" "This habit is going to be the worse of me" "I will struggle with this problem for a long time" "It is just who I am". These are confessions to self that are as a result of negative thoughts, if the effect stopped at just words, one wouldn't be so worried, but it doesn't.

The negative words give way for a very lackluster personality that isn't willing to do anything about a situation. If you struggled with being fit, the negative perception causes you to become lazy.

If you wanted to quit a habit, you would lack the motivation to take the right steps, and the circle continues for anyone who wouldn't kick out negative thinking. The connection between the mind and personality is so strong; you cannot afford to fill your account with the wrong stuff while hoping for the best personality traits. Most striking is the fact that your thoughts become the compass through which you can make progress with discipline.

Strengthen your self-discipline today with positive thoughts, and you will not have to deal with a negative personality. Some people take the right steps towards being self-disciplined; they have a manual of sorts on the subject but cannot reconcile what is written with their life experiences because their personality isn't just right.

The personality issue can be handled by being focused on what you think about the most, what are those thoughts you take to bed with you and the ones you rise within the morning? You've got to be aware of your thinking pattern; it is the only way you can toughen up your personality.

Let the words you say to yourself be a source of encouragement to you on this journey, so this means you've got to fuel your mind with great thoughts that aid the right personality and help you attain self-discipline.

Positive Thinking and Discipline

If you have discussed with a goldsmith, you will discover that the process of creating gold trinkets and pieces of jewelry is a very long one that entails taking the gold substance through fire.

Until gold goes through the fire, it will never be fully formed. Think about self-discipline as gold (what you desire right now) and positive thinking as the fire it must go through to attain perfection.

Self-discipline can be enhanced with positive thinking; you have a responsibility to train yourself by going through the rigorous process of selecting your thoughts.

A person who can fight negative thoughts and win can become a disciplined individual. It takes a lot of self-control to filter your thinking pattern, but you must be committed to this all-important process.

The Cure to Laziness (This Could Change Your Life)

As you strive you think positively, you are also training yourself in the discipline; this is the major idea behind self-discipline and positive thinking. Just like gold, it will take a while for your mind to adjust to a consistent line of thought.

Even when it feels like you have "Arrived" and you are making progress, negative thoughts still try to creep into your mind. The process of kicking out the negative to maintain the positive is likened to building up resistance for self-discipline.

As you fight off negative thoughts, you will also be building up the ability to fight off that bad habit, addiction, problem or challenge that makes it difficult for you to attain self-discipline.

If you always used to think that it was impossible for you to lose weight (this is just an example) before trying to actually "Lose" weight through exercise and dieting, you need to start by replacing the "Can't" with "Can".

Every time the thought of being able to lose weight pops in your head, get rid of it. As you remove the view from your mind, tell yourself that you can do it and start thinking about doing it.

Now, this process will go on for a while, even when you start a diet, negative thoughts remind you that it is possible for you to relapse. The more you get rid of the evil thoughts that weigh you down, the stronger you feel towards achieving your goals, and this is what sets you on course towards being self-disciplined. For some people, they fight off the thought at the initial stages but give in to the temptation of believing the negative ideas.

Gradually such persons begin to doubt their abilities, they don't believe what they can do, and this negative outlook becomes their reality. For people to become stable with their thoughts, they must take proactive measures towards monitoring what they think about.

A person doesn't get to think positive thoughts suddenly, the same way gold doesn't sparkle and shine without going through the fire. There must be a combination of effort and consistency for positive thinking to become a part of a person's mental routine. When a pattern is established in mind, the real battle begins.

Winning the Battle of The Mind

If you succeed with infusing positivity into your thinking process, you have overcome the first challenge with the mind, but there is still so much to do because now, you will be compelled to fight the battle of the mind.

Let's go back to our conversation on gold, shall we? Getting the gold substance itself isn't a guarantee that the goldsmith has got something substantial, yes, it is valuable as gold but what can be made from it? What are the assurances that when made into a piece of jewelry it's going to last long?

The Cure to Laziness (This Could Change Your Life)

So, the gold must go through the fire first. Until the product is tried and tested, there will be doubts and questions. Fire here symbolizes the battle of the mind; everyone who seeks to perfect self-discipline through possible thoughts must win the battle over negative thinking.

Every day presents an opportunity for you to decide and make choices; the process of choosing something over another is where the battle starts to unfold.

If a person has been dealing with pornographic addiction but has been trying to maintain self-discipline through positive thinking, he/she must face the battle of the mind when the temptation to watch porn surfaces.

If the person gives in to the temptation, then it means the battle is lost to negative forces, and self-discipline (which is the prize) cannot be gained at that time. If he/she wins, it translates into a stronger positive mind that can resist porn until the temptation doesn't pop up again.

So what battle are you faced with? Is it the battle of procrastination? Fear of the unknown? Weight loss? Whatever it is, you can win the contest! However, you must have the right tools, and by devices, we are referring to positive thoughts.

Train your mind to reject negative suggestions instantaneously, don't give such thoughts any space or the luxury of time to brood over it.

When you start cutting off little problematic ideas, you will be strengthening and preparing yourself for the larger battle which is often at the decision-making stage.

Some people have remained undisciplined despite reading books and listening to podcasts about how to become self-disciplined not because they were born that way but because they haven't activated the power of their mind.

Now is a great time to start processing positive thoughts, here is a tip you can try out; every night before you sleep; have a rundown of your thought process for the entire day.

If there were negative thoughts, fight them off and replace them immediately with positive thoughts. If you do this daily, you will be repositioning your mind rightly.

Self-discipline can be achieved when a person takes control of his/her mind using a positive thought process. The battle of the mind is real, but you can win with consistent practice, focus and a residue of positive images to replace every negative thought that crosses your mind.

It's All Inside of You!
The most fantastic concept about using thoughts to establish self-discipline is the fact that everything you need to make it happen is

within you. You have the most incredible superpower of all time; your mind!

You don't have to rely on anyone else to help you think the right thoughts, come on; it is YOUR mind and your journey towards being self-disciplined. So, you've got to learn how to rely on yourself and bring out so many good thoughts which help you grow from a struggling positive thinker to a stable one.

With some other ideas on how to become self-disciplined, you might require help from someone who will aid your success, but with positive thinking, you are 100% responsible for how it all turns out.

Being fully responsible for your progress means you have more work to do, but it also presents an opportunity for you to remodel your thoughts such that they align with your decision to become a self-disciplined individual. However, you must believe that you've got what it takes; things tend to work better with your plans for discipline when you have faith in yourself.

Regardless of what you are dealing with in your personal life, it is possible to get solutions through positive thoughts. Wake up every morning determined to do better with your thinking process; create images of the successes you enjoy when you start to exhibit self-discipline. These images will serve as alternative materials after you fight off a negative thought.

You want to become better; you want to be the best version of yourself, but you must be self-disciplined first. This means that your involvement is required at every stage. A determined mind doesn't feel inadequate, yes you may struggle at first, but if you hold on to your thought process and belief on how this works for you, there will be progress at the end of the experience.

The entire focus is on you because no one else can "Think" for you, nobody can take your negative thoughts and turn them around. You are also the only one who knows exactly what you think about, and the challenges you are trying to deal with so being the captain of the situation is crucial.

Another reason why you are at the center of this concept is that you are the only one who can be passionate enough to desire changes in your life. It is called "Self-discipline" for a reason, meaning it is all about YOU!

A vital lesson you should get from this chapter is that the power to transform your life lies within you. There are no extra lessons, mentoring sessions or professional help, just you and your thoughts making it through all the negativity and winning.

Be present with your thoughts, never allow yourself to go with a flow of views that are mostly negative. So that means you should be aware of how you think; when it becomes negative, replace it with positive,

The Cure to Laziness (This Could Change Your Life)

continue with the process until you achieve a sustainable result with your goals.

If you have always struggled with anything in life, it is because you didn't handle it from within first using your thoughts. Have you ever thought about a person and boom, the person shows up right before you or calls you? It might feel strange at the time, but this is just an example of the power of thoughts.

You can be a self-disciplined person who becomes a source of inspiration to others by fixating your thought process On things that are positive. Positivity yields optimism, even in the face of challenges, you press on knowing that things will get better.

Self-discipline that is obtained through positive thinking is sustainable because it becomes a way of life for you. You get to the point where you no longer struggle with that bad habit; you experience profound changes gradually because everything on the inside of you is correctly aligned with positivity.

You can win the battle against negative thinking, but you must be intentional about it by protecting your mind. Believe in your ability to become a self-disciplined person, trust the process and only accept the best thoughts about yourself.

Identify the events, activities, words and people that trigger negative vibes around, and within you, after identification, you must create a plan that enables you to get rid of the negative indicators (especially the people in that category).

Self-discipline will become a reality when you deal with the challenge of getting rid of negative thoughts. With this process appropriately handled, you can proceed to the next idea which presents a connection between self-discipline and weight loss.

Chapter 6:
The Secret of Self-Discipline and Entrepreneur

"This quality of self-denial in pursuit of a longer-term goal and, indeed, the willpower to maintain the denial, is excellent training for the boardroom." - John Viney

One of the best and highest honors anyone can bestow upon himself is self-discipline. It is the ability of the mind to dictate and control the body, with the heart as a guiding light, leading the way. Self-discipline involves being able to set your heart on something and stick to it religiously, in the face of temptation and distractions. It can be as simple as waking up early, to sticking to only two cups of alcohol per day, to paying a monthly visit to your aged parents.

Self-discipline is not negotiable for an entrepreneur. It should form the basis of your character and guide you to success. You might be lucky to experience short term success when you start a business. This is likely to happen if your product appeals to customers and you are knowledgeable about the business. However, the spice that will keep this success going is self-discipline.

Key Self-Discipline Tactics for Entrepreneurial Success

Many businesses have failed today as a result of a lack of self-discipline, coupled with the right mindset. Maybe failure is an extreme word, but many businesses perform way below their capacity due to an inability of the management to apply due discipline in the needed areas. Many people come up with great ideas, yet they hardly survive and develop effectively to compete.

It is a beautiful thing to be an entrepreneur, however, the word self – discipline is what separates the successful from the unsuccessful. Any business endeavor has many huge and vital components encompassing it. It takes discipline to commit to diligently studying the various areas/segment and committing to it.

In starting a business, many people feel the hardest part is having an idea worth investing in, while the easier part is executing this advice. However, the reverse is the case. There are entrepreneurs out there with terrific ideas. They were brave enough to birth their ideas into business but lack the discipline to grow the business and see it through thick and thin.

This baffles me since building a business is not a herculean task. In this regard, here are some areas of self-discipline that an entrepreneur can apply for business success. The following discusses some discipline you need to apply as an entrepreneur.

Developing A Marketing Plan to Generate A Steady Income Stream

There should be a selling point about your product or services that stands it out from the competition. It is this selling point that you capitalize on when you are trying to advertise which gives you a competitive advantage and a unique selling point.

You should be disciplined enough to offer your customers a benefit that no other ones will. If your business is offering services, for instance, be sure that your services take care of the unique needs of individuals and businesses you will be offering your services to, as no two individual/business are the same. It takes self-discipline to identify this.

Self-Discipline Will Help You to Be Proactive

You can either function through crisis mode or put down modalities to ensure that your business doesn't get dragged into the crisis. What are the proactive measures you have in place to make sure your goal becomes a reality? It is with discipline that you get to adjust early and be able to foresee crisis ahead rather than being reactive to a crisis.

It takes self-discipline with the right mindset to be intentional about your business. Else, you risk crisis and other horrible surprises as well as missing beautiful opportunities.

Self-Discipline to Focus on The Most Important Things Only

You can be so busy with activities yet having nothing tangible to show forth. It takes the right mindset to focus on the right time management practice which will keep you on track and prevent you from getting distracted by low or no value activities. When you define your desired outcome, you will be able to take the necessary steps towards bringing this to reality.

There are project management tools that can help you effectively manage the task, and ultimately manage your time. This keeps your focus on the essentials, keeping you and the team on track. There are also automated processes that can help get rid of distractions.

It Takes Discipline to Think in The Long-Term

Successful businesses are built on relationships. This takes time as the progression will go from 'know' to 'like' and finally 'trust'. A long-term perspective for your business is a sure recipe for success. It, however, takes discipline to let go of instant gratifications in terms of ventures that are not worth investing in.

It Takes Self-Discipline to Take Some Timeout

Establishing a business is a demanding feature that takes time and energy. It is easy to get carried away and neglect family, friends, and even yourself. To be successful, this is non-negotiable. The best part, however, is that entrepreneurship is the only line of job that gives you freedom.

With discipline, you know when to detach yourself from work. Also, self-discipline makes you know when you need to take a step back and catch up with your friends, family and loved ones.

It Takes Discipline to Remain Motivated and Strive for Development

It is vital for entrepreneurs to maintain their motivation. As an entrepreneur, you have got to create and encourage challenges to keep you on your toes and maintain motivation. Also, it takes self-discipline not to relent on your knowledge. Rather, you strive for more knowledge and experience via seminars and refresher courses. With this, you stay current, keep abreast of happenings in your field, which will put you in a good place to drive your business to success.

Self-Discipline Helps Maintain A Team

The importance of teamwork for any business venture cannot be overemphasized. It is vital for any business setting to work in sync. When an entrepreneur encourages teamwork, you can leverage all the talents from your workforce. This will allow you to improve productivity, improve quality and efficiency.

A team activity is like a motor vehicle engine. The various parts of the engines need to work in sync for the vehicle to operate seamlessly.

Daily Self-Discipline Tips for The Entrepreneurs

Anyone can come up with beautiful business ideas. However, staying true and committed to the idea does not come on a platter of gold.

This is what makes successful entrepreneurs stand out. If you take a critical look at successful entrepreneurs, I am pretty sure, they are people that have mastered the art of self-discipline and trained their mindset along the way.

Starting a business is easy, anyone can do that. However, maintaining the business and committing to it such that it stands the test of time is not something that comes naturally. It takes resilience, determination with the right mindset to see a business endeavor to the top.

This doesn't happen in a day, neither does it come in a month. Your success as an entrepreneur is the cumulative effect of all your efforts since inception. In other words, all your inputs affect the success of your enterprise, directly or indirectly.

Since your success as an entrepreneur is a factor of your daily input, it is important to develop the right attitude and mindset essential for success. Here are tips that should be applied daily to bring you nearer to your goal and improve productivity.

1. Don't Get Caught Up with Perfectionism

We understand there is no singular way to execute a project. Hence, when you complete any project, resist the urge to beat yourself up on ways to make it better. When you complete a project, there is a big possibility that a fresh burst of ideas come rushing at you on ways to make or improve the project.

Without self-discipline, you might find yourself starting all over again, leaving you swamped and rushing to meet the deadline. Learn to step back and restrict yourself. It is not as hard as it seems.

2. Keep The 80/20 Rule in Mind

This is known as the Pareto principle or the law of vital few, which states that for many events, about 80% of the effect comes from 20% of the causes. In a business sense, it states that people in a business devote 80% of their time and effort on irrelevancies, and 20% on the important ones.

It takes self-discipline to sit down and realize the truly important task. And even the less important ones can be outsourced or automated. This will allow you to focus on important things which will make your business better off.

3. Dedicate Time to Preparation

It is not all about having your to-do list and schedule for the day. Form the habit of examining it critically and dedicating enough time for each activity. This should not be an excuse to procrastinate, rather, an avenue to reflect and ensure you have all grounds covered.

Be sure to organize your schedule and to-do list in relation to your goal. This little act that sounds rather insignificant can improve your productivity.

4. Detach Your Feelings from The Equation

It takes self-discipline to be able to separate emotions from your enterprise. Many people are so controlled by their emotions and feelings that they wouldn't attempt any task until they feel like it. This is one of the characteristics of procrastination which doesn't have to be so.

There is a big chance that you might never really feel like attempting a task. In this case, what you need is the motivation and zeal to overcome the inertia to get started. Once you begin, you will realize that you just flow along with it. With self-discipline and the right mindset, you can master these emotions and get hold of yourself.

5. Master the Art of Negotiating

As an entrepreneur, this is one of the skills you must really master before you enter the business world. This skill will allow you to get sweet deals on offers and set you up for maximum profit. Besides, it takes discipline to separate emotions from negotiations and business deals. This way, with the right mindset, you will not feel guilty when you negotiate lower prices on your purchases, and you offer high prices when selling. Although, it also takes self-discipline not to offer your services at a price that will be uncomfortable for your customers which might end up backfiring.

6. Develop Mental Toughness

Shall we face it; no one plans for failures, losses, and setbacks in business. However, no matter how proactive and smart you claim to be, these things are sometimes inevitable. This is where resilience, one of the attributes of self-discipline will help you get back on your feet and keep you going.

Your setback could be minimal, and others so huge and it seems like the end of the world. Here is where your stability in the face of a crisis that you have developed through self-discipline coupled with the right mindset will be of great help in helping you survive the storms of the business world.

7. Take Care of Yourself

It is so easy to get caught up in late night meetings. Skipping breakfast is not new to you since you are not so attentive to listen to the rumblings of your stomach. It is easy to work late into the night all in a bid to close the deal and meet the deadline. Many see vacation as a luxury they cannot afford. Yet, all this happens at the expense of your health.

This is where self-discipline comes in. You have got to know when to take a step back and relax. Do away with the stress that comes with running a business. Starting or keeping a business running is very tasking, which makes it so easy to be carried away at the expense of your health. Be sure to take your meals on time, take vacations when due and learn to leave everything work related at work.

In rounding up this chapter, bear in mind that as an entrepreneur, your success depends on a lot of factors/recipes. However, I want you to see self-discipline as the glue that binds all other recipes together. Hence, even with the best employee, a kick-ass idea, unbreakable team spirit, beautiful foresight and first-class training, without discipline, your enterprise is a disaster waiting to happen.

Chapter 7:
Secret to Self-Discipline and Addiction, Procrastination and Laziness

"Willpower is what separates us from the animals. It's the capacity to restrain our impulses, resist temptation – do what's right and good for us in the long run, not what we want to do right now. It's central, in fact, to civilization." - Dr. Roy Baumeister, Ph.D.

One thing many people with negative vices all acknowledge is the fact that in them lies the power and strength to change their lives for the better. However, due to one thing or the other, they assume and believe that they are not capable of bringing forth that change. This, however, is not so as the major key is to keep working on yourself, overcoming the challenges you meet such that in the future, you look back and are glad of the decision you made.

You don't start and tackle a problem as big as it is. Be specific about your goals and think about the best ways to make it come to reality. A die-hard drunk, for instance, is deceiving himself if he totally cuts himself off from alcohol consumption. He needs to reduce the quantity gradually until he can live safely without being bothered by the cravings. Habits are not formed overnight hence, breaking free of them takes a process – a long, painful and sometimes boring process. This is where the place of self-discipline with the right mindset comes in. Self-discipline will keep you in track when every fiber of your being is crying at you to relapse.

Keep in mind that breaking free from bad habits requires some form of sacrifice. However, I will advise you not to think of it as letting go of something. Addiction to food, nicotine, and porn, etc., pleasures certain parts of the brain. When you are a diehard addict, it is difficult to let go. You will feel you can't get through the day without it.

This is not surprising as humans tend to get comfortable in these vices. They form a comfort zone around these habits hence trying to do away with it doesn't augur well. This is where the power of self-discipline with the right mindset comes in. In breaking free, you need goals and a strategy to achieve your goal. It is self-discipline that will keep you on track when you feel like losing it, and you feel like the walls are crashing down on you.

No matter how difficult it might seem, you can break free. The power lies in you to train your brain and mind to move towards your aim and achieve it. With the power of self-discipline coupled with the right attitude, you can be successful.

With the above in mind, I will discuss powerful strategies to break free from addiction, procrastination, and laziness. We will leverage the power of self-discipline with the right mindset.

Self-Discipline and Breaking Free from Addiction

Breaking free from addiction is more than being determined. Whatever method you choose to break free of your vice, self-discipline is very vital to success. Your goal might be freedom from excess sugar, stopping nicotine use, stopping porn or other substance abuse. While this is possible, long-term success only comes on the wing of self-discipline.

Self-control, one of the important characters you must develop to break free of addiction, also depends on self-discipline. While self-control has more to do about the present, self-discipline allows you to feel the impact of self-control over time.

Self-control will help you make a more rational decision. It will prevent the emotional weight of any situation from influencing your decision making. This explains the ability of people to dissociate stress or other external impulses from inflicting their decision making. This boils back to self-discipline.

Self-discipline is a habit that is learned through determination, dedication, and practice. While it is easy to think that self-discipline will help you through recovery, self-discipline is a habit you must develop and make it stronger and part of you with time.

Self-Discipline and Breaking Free from Addiction

Breaking free from addiction is more than being determined. Whatever method you choose to break free of your vice, self-discipline is very vital to success. Your goal might be freedom from excess sugar, stopping nicotine use, stopping porn or other substance abuse. While this is possible, long-term success only comes on the wing of self-discipline.

Self-control, one of the important characters you must develop to break free of addiction, also depends on self-discipline. While self-control has more to do about the present, self-discipline allows you to feel the impact of self-control over time.

Self-control will help you make a more rational decision. It will prevent the emotional weight of any situation from influencing your decision making. This explains the ability of people to dissociate stress or other external impulses from inflicting their decision making. This boils back to self-discipline.

Self-discipline is a habit that is learned through determination, dedication, and practice. While it is easy to think that self-discipline will help you through recovery, self-discipline is a habit you must develop and make it stronger and part of you with time.

How to Develop Self-Discipline in Recovery?

For people trying to break from the shackles of substance abuse, porn or any vice, self-discipline is not negotiable. It is a vital key to making the journey to self-recovery easy hence guaranteeing a happy and fulfilled life.

Avoid the Triggers

Getting rid of triggers in the form of temptation is crucial to staying sober. The best way is to stay away from triggers. This can come in many forms depending on your type of addiction. Getting rid of all the bottles of alcohols from your fridge, and nicotine, and staying away from some friends for instance, takes determination.

Recovering addicts need the will and discipline to decline outings with old friends. Peer pressure is real and difficult. But making a choice to be rigid and unwavering is critical in the journey to sobriety.

Eat Healthy

Many people struggling with substance abuse often neglect themselves and make horrible food choices. Yet the eating habit has a lot to do about the kind of decision you make. Hence, when in recovery, it is important to commit to healthy meal choices.

This is because there is a link between healthy food and staying sober. With low blood sugar, it is easy to have a foul mood and make poor decisions. Be sure to eat well and see your mealtime as an opportunity to strengthen self-discipline. It will help build resilience that will help with the recovery process.

Embrace The "Wrong"

Over time, excessive dependency on the substance of abuse has reconfigured the brain of the Addict. Hence, he/she sees nothing wrong in a bottle of champagne or cigarette every now and then. Thus, giving in to the demands and cravings of the addiction feels naturally right. However, in the journey to sobriety, there must be a reconfiguration of the brain. This is because the brain thrives based on habits.

As a result of this, you must be willing to work with the "wrong" in your journey to recovery. Since you are incorporating a new set of habits, it might be uncomfortable. This is where self-discipline to stay on track comes in. Humans are wired to hate changes. Hence, your system might rebel against this new-found way of life. With time, practice, consistency and self-discipline, you can retrain your mind to do what is right.

Stay Away from New Addictions

People, in a bid to stay away from addiction, are prone to developing other ones fast. In a bid to fill the void left by sex, porn, or alcohol, they might replace it with excessive eating, nicotine or a variety of other activities.

Herein lies the power of self-discipline. It is with self-discipline and great inner strength that an addict can remain strong and apply moderation to all sectors of their life.

Put Your Thoughts in Order

There is a direct relation between conscious thoughts, stress level and consequent cravings. Most recovering addicts are taught this so that when they get back to the society, they consciously reflect on their self to block every avenue of negative thoughts that could trigger stress which might bring up the addiction.

Stress will arise as you go about your daily activities. There will be people, situations and circumstances to deal with. While you have no power over this, you have every power over your thoughts and with self-control; you can stay positive and keep cravings at bay.

How Self-Discipline Helps with Procrastination

Before we discuss this, it is vital to understand what procrastination is. Procrastination is a habit that arises from a lack of self-control. It arises when our self-control is too low or inadequate to push us to accomplish our goal. We set out to do something, but we do not have the will to overcome the inertia to get the project started.

It is best to see procrastination as a problem, a problem that relates to self-control and self-discipline. It is that lack of self-control that will make it difficult to get the motivation to accomplish what you set out to. Hence, you only find yourself planning to wake up early, to meditate, and to go to the gym. You just cannot seem to get yourself to start out the task. But why do we procrastinate? We lack self-discipline and self-control, it's that simple!

Hence, in fighting procrastination, we need to get to the root of the matter and build up our self-control. A disciplined life is the only tested solution to break the habit. There is no secret formula or magic to help you do away with procrastination.

Since procrastination is a failure in controlling yourself and giving yourself the needed push to overcome work inertia, you need self-control and discipline. It is when you get better at self-control that you will able to get rid of procrastination. Self-control is built with the power and strength of a disciplined life.

How Can You Make Your Life More Disciplined?

Get up early and deactivate the snooze button (if possible), go for a run, make healthy food choices and live a mindful life. When your life is disciplined, your self-control improves, ultimately getting rid of procrastination will be easy. Hence, one of the major keys to beat procrastination is to improve on your willpower. You can develop this by engaging in a minute task every day such as daily meditation, doing the dishes after a meal, making your bed once you get up, and reading a book rather than being on social media. In dealing with procrastination, leveraging on the power of self-discipline, I have these crucial points in understanding and avoiding it.

Identify Excuses and Stop Them

The Cure to Laziness (This Could Change Your Life)

Although not everyone might want to admit it, we all make excuses. Yet, if you do want to get rid of procrastination in your life, you must admit this.

It will have been better if it had stopped at making excuses, but we justify these accuses, allowing the brain to interpret it as normal. We have become so clever and creative that we develop legitimate reasons why we cannot commit to our obligation.

If you will, however, break free from the shackles of procrastination, you must identify and get rid of excuses. Again, it comes back to our sincerity in separating legitimate reasons from mere excuses.

Your Self-Discipline Will Reflect in Your Choices

Someone once said we are a product of our choices. This is one of the attributes peculiar to man. Every blessed day, right from when we open our eyes in the morning, we are faced with choices of whether to wake up or keep sleeping, the type of food to eat, what to wear and whether to meditate or not.

We go about the various task of the day following routines and doing the same thing over and over. Once weekly obligations are done with, we see our free time as a time to our self. This is where the issue lies. The little free time we can get at the end of the day or after each workday, we make sure we dedicate it to relaxation. This is where we leave off other essential things we must do. We put them off and make excuses. Hence, rather than finish the tax report, we will curl up on the sofa and catch up with our favorite football club game.

- This pattern of thinking and lifestyle has got to stop!

To completely rid yourself of procrastination, you need to leverage the power of choice, which still boils down to self-discipline. It is self-discipline that will compel you not to relax and try to reward yourself with "irrelevancies" at the expense of what you really must do.

- You can hit the snooze button, wake up thirty minutes later and rush to work only to fumble at your presentation, or do it right.

- You can fill your intestine with candies, sweet and other sugar-laden substance and deal with obesity and diabetes later or eat healthily and be rewarded with optimum health.

- You can play Xbox all week, crash read and perform woefully at the end of the semester test, or study through the week and get good grades.

- Choices!

Effectively using the power of choices is one way to get rid of procrastination. With self-discipline as your driving force, you can commit to developing your mind, going for a workout, dedicating time to the project etc. You build your self-control and ultimately break free from the grip of procrastination!

Find Your Motivation

No matter how hard you try to do away with excuses, how determined you are to invest your choices wisely, without the right motivation, your effort to do away with procrastination might not stand the test of time.

Hence, a self-disciplined mindset, with the motivation to close a deal will keep a salesman up all night fine-tuning his sales pitch, rather than assuming one way or the other, everything will work out fine.

Bearing the above in mind, you have got to be diligent enough to find your motivation. A student needs the motivation of good grades to keep studying, burning the midnight oil and doing everything necessary to ensure academic success. The motivation of an aspiring Olympic athlete to win a gold medal will keep him on his toes, practicing through thick and thin, when comfortable or not to prepare himself for the event.

When self-discipline is combined with motivation, you are guaranteed to put out the fire of procrastination with ease.

Commence Gradually

Habits are not developed overnight hence; it is foolhardy thinking you can do away with procrastination overnight. You have got to start small and start gradually and take it easy with yourself. Unless your self-control is at its peak, you are bound for failure if you jump at it.

Slowly and steadily, let your life revolve around that healthy habit you want to incorporate. With your motivation and self-discipline, watch as you grow stronger and become rigid in that habit.

Getting free from the shackles of procrastination is a gradual process. With the right weapons in your arsenal, however, you can fast track your way to success and take control of your life. If you find your motivation, self-discipline will keep you going despite all odds.

Self-Discipline and Overcoming Laziness

Humans have this inborn attitude to always seek the easy way out. This expresses itself in the form of laziness when people outrightly shy away from activities. Yet, laziness can become an embargo to your productivity and overall success if appropriate measures are not taken to curb it.

Laziness is an attitude that we all must deal with, especially if we want to go far in life. It is a battle that can serve as a clog in the wheel of progress of anyone. Luckily, the fact that you are on this eBook means you are ready to overcome laziness. Here are some tested tips to overcome laziness:

Think of The Long-Term Effect

When you think about what you stand to gain or lose from doing or not doing a task, it can help make the right decision. The psychological effect of being lazy can serve as an inspiration for getting on your feet and face your task head-on.

The Cure to Laziness (This Could Change Your Life)

This is an effective method because the mind makes better decisions when aware of the long-term effect of any activity. This is an effective strategy that gears people who set goals to do all in their capacity to bring it to realization.

If you can visualize what you stand to gain, how accomplishing your task will make you better off, you have given your mind the needed passion and zeal to get into action. This is a technique that can help clip laziness in its wings for good in your life. That is not all, read on.

Break Your Tasks into Bits

One of the reasons people become lazy is due to the overwhelming nature of the task ahead. Hence, there is this inertia that they can't seem to get rid of. Even with much self-discipline, strenuous activities could be pretty discouraging. This discouragement produces a sort of psychological effect on the brain, where the natural balance is disturbed.

In a bid to restore sanity, the brain would suggest that you put off the task. This is where laziness sets in. The best way to constructively counter this is to divide the tasks into bits. Let yourself know that you will not tackle it at a stretch.

For instance, I read a book on intermittent fasting some time back. The book talked about not eating for about eight hours at a stretch. Everything in me cried against this. However, when I got to the portion that recommended taking water and other forms of juice, I was relieved. Also, the portion that advised I can start with a 5 hour fast and gradually extend the hours was a big encouragement.

In the same way, confronting your task this way reduces the tendency of being overwhelmed which could help curb laziness.

Reduce Distractions

There are so many distractions (for instance social media) vying for our attention that committing on a task is usually hard. While advancement in tech has been a blessing, it has its fair share in contributing to people's laziness.

This is because there is pressure to keep up with social media, update status or impress people with social media pictures and posts. This is where discipline comes in. Centuries ago for instance when there were minimal distractions, productivity was high, reducing the tendency to have divided attention.

To deal with laziness, one of the most effective tips is to cut off other unproductive activities that compete for your time. This explains why specialists would advise you to stay away from the TV for the rest of your life and kill your social media activities. While this might be extreme, the best approach is to minimize distractions.

How Do You Reduce Distractions?

Have a leisure time: The distraction to keep up with social media contributes to laziness and affects productivity. While deactivating social media accounts sounds extreme, we recommend you have a scheduled time. This is where the self-discipline to resist the urge to check FB notification comes in.

Have a Not-to-do list: You're not-to-do list a list of all activities that are an embargo to the fulfillment of your task. For instance, it is not practical to write that you will visit your old parents today. Rather, make a list of all activities that could prevent you from visiting your parents. Hence, you can say: I will not take a nap today or, I will not spend more than two hours on my PC.

The idea behind a not-to-do list is to see clearly the things that compete for your time. These are likely to prevent you from committing to the task at hand. Identifying this helps put you on the path of success to curb laziness.

Avoid Being Too Hard on Yourself

You admit you could be lazy, and you are on a quest to get help, terrific!

You have seen how laziness has cost you and you are out to overcome it. However, you get disappointed at times when you fall short. This might be pretty discouraging when it happens, and you try to beat yourself up for falling short of expectation.

In contrast to being hard on yourself and beating yourself up, I advise that you attempt something else. Praise yourself; give yourself kudos for the efforts. The brain is likely to respond effectively and be motivated to positive reinforcement rather than scolding yourself. Whenever you fall short of expectations, be sure to attempt this.

Cultivate Self-Discipline

In trying to overcome laziness, I will use this illustration to show the impact of self-discipline. Consider all the efforts and tips listed above as all the parts of a motor vehicle engine. Look at self-discipline as the engine oil that keeps every other part running smoothly and in order. Without engine oil, a vehicle engine is headed for destruction.

In other words, the tendency of all the tips discussed above to produce a result is very low if not accompanied by self-discipline. It is self-discipline that can help you think in the long-term. It is self-discipline that will allow you to put off distractions, schedule a time for social media, and abide by it religiously. It is only self-discipline that can help you leave instant gratification and think of the long-term effect and consequences of your actions and choices.

You can overcome laziness. It will, however, happen on the wings of self-discipline, coupled with the right mindset.

Chapter 8:
The Secret to Self-Discipline and Weight Loss

"Willpower is the key to success. Successful people strive no matter what they feel by applying their will to overcome apathy, doubt or fear." - Dan Millman

The desire to lose weight tops the list of what most people want which inspires them to become self-disciplined. Aside from the thrill of having a sexy body, there are a lot of health benefits to be gained from losing weight, but it wouldn't happen without consistent effort.

People who struggle endlessly with weight loss do not have an organized plan of action; they want to lose weight, they want to do whatever it takes to achieve their goal, but because of the absence of organization, their wishes are not attained.

It takes a lot of self-discipline for a person to start the process of weight loss and continue in it even after they get to their desired weight because fitness should be a significant aspect of everyone's life. You shouldn't consider weight loss only when you want to shed some pounds, make it a permanent part of your life.

In a previous chapter, there was a section on habits and how those routine activities you do affect the quality of your life. From that chapter, you gained insight into how you can create better practices and the same message resonates in this section as well.

Until you intentionally incorporate the right habits into your life, your weight loss idea will be nothing but a dream.

While the central focus of this chapter isn't on patterns, you should have the concept in mind as you read because, in the end, you must adjust with your habits for sustained weight loss experience.

Habits are a part of you, but plans are ideas you should implement that will help you achieve your goals. For you to be self-disciplined, you need a combination of habits and methods. So, what can you do?

Firstly, you should get an organized plan that will help you keep track of your purpose and then make these plans a part of your habit by doing them repeatedly.

Being able to lose weight through regular exercise is a plan, using the staircase at the office instead of the elevator can become a habit inspired by the initial idea to exercise regularly.

When there is an agreement between your plans and habits, self-discipline becomes possible. You wouldn't struggle to go to the gym, eat

The Cure to Laziness (This Could Change Your Life)

healthy, stay off calories or eat in portions. All of these can be adequately managed using the principles of time maximization.

Manage Your Time

Even when you start to make plans a part of your habit, if you are not conscious of how to use time, you will still have issues. One of the secrets to being self-disciplined and lose weight is to use time wisely; you will not get an extra minute, second or hour.

Everyone has the same amount of time yet why do some people make progress more than others?

The reason you feel lazy and too tired to head to the gym in the morning is probably because you didn't use your time well the previous day which is why you went to bed late. So, every time you don't use your time wisely, there is a ripple effect of your inaction snowballing into the rest of the day.

Taking charge of your time isn't just to lose weight, yes this is what you want to achieve now, but there is so much more than you can do with proper time management. As you lose weight, you will also observe that there are other significant changes taking place in your life simultaneously.

But back to weight loss, you can achieve your goal with effective time management; Don't do the things that aid weight loss when it is convenient for you, your goal should propel you to schedule your time, making room for important activities that bring you closer to your dream.

A daily planner will be handy at this point, sit down the day before a new day and plan. Set time aside for the regular things you do (your job, family time) and then create a separate schedule for the weight loss activities you want to do for that day.

For example, plan to wake up in the morning and go for a run, drink water, take a healthy breakfast, get to work and use the stairs. At lunchtime, enjoy veggies and get back home in the evening for some yoga. Have an early dinner and turn in early for sleep as well.

With a plan, you know exactly what to do every time, and you are motivated to doing it because the activities are interwoven with every other action lined up for your day.

Your ability to schedule your time and stick to the plan is a testament of your growth with being self-disciplined. Set a specific target for yourself; when do you want to lose weight? How many pounds do you want to drop? What can you do weekly that brings you closer to the milestone?

You will carry out weight loss tasks with a sense of urgency when you have precise objectives to attain. It is your responsibility to achieve the goals you set on this journey to fitness and health. How does a person become responsible for their life?

The Cure to Laziness (This Could Change Your Life)

Take 100 Percent Responsibility for Your Life

Did you know that it is possible to have the answers to weight loss and not make as much progress as you desire? Oh, it is possible, and it isn't because of anything you did wrong, sometimes it's just a function of your body.

Some people will complain, scream and murmur about their inability to shed weight at a breakneck pace. As they complain, they try to lay the blame on someone or something else, their nutritionist, the food, gym instructor, their boss, etc.

Complaining and blaming others isn't a sign of being responsible, it just shows how undisciplined you are. You've got to take 100% responsibility for your life today!

Things will go well with you sometimes, and then they may not go well with you some other times, in good or bad seasons, you are responsible for your life. Do not resort to complaints that do not change anything, don't blame the world of its system for issues you can resolve.

One of the hallmarks of self-disciplined individuals is their ability to stay calm when their dreams don't happen the way they want it to. Such persons realize that if something isn't working, they can improve on it instead of grumble about it.

You are the custodian of your dream and society will not be held responsible should that dream wither away. Get yourself together, be bold to face challenges with a solution-oriented mind. It is easier to complain about something that isn't working than to act on it, but the pathway to greatness is never secure.

Responsibility births self-discipline; start to do the things required of you without anyone forcing you to do them and regardless of the outcome, keeping working at it.

Being responsible also helps you identify your areas of weakness, maybe you've not been going to the gym because you don't like the treadmill.

Well, when you take responsibility for your results (when they are negative), it causes you to reflect on what went wrong. Upon discovering that you don't like the treadmill, you can change it and stick to what you want.

Don't complain when faced with challenges, discipline your mind to provide solutions if problems spring up. Placing the blame on someone else or an institution is irresponsible.

Responsibility also comes with awareness; you become conscious of the fact that everything you have achieved can be replicated into the future. This means you need to consider long-term plans.

Think Long-Term

The people you admire who exhibit self-discipline weren't born that way, and they certainly didn't attain the level of discipline they show by sticking to routines occasionally.

Convenience and pleasure are two ideas that will affect your journey to being self-disciplined if you don't handle them early enough. Long-term dreams are not done conveniently; they are also not done when there is time or when you "Can", you do them because you NEED to.

More so, doing things out of pleasure will not help you lose weight, neither will it make you a self-disciplined person. People who focus on what gives them pleasure forfeit their progress for a short-term feeling.

The fact that you love pizza and the spicy sensation it gives doesn't mean you should take it every day especially if you want to lose weight. The feeling pizza gives you is short-term, it probably wouldn't exceed 24 hours - is this short experience worth the entire dream to lose weight?

You have an opportunity to build something sustainable from today by acting in alignment with your long-term goals. It doesn't matter if you love potato chips so much, so long as it isn't healthy for you, don't indulge it. Always think about how you want to be in the future, create an image in your mind and hold on it.

The next time you are tempted to decide based on short-term gratification, remember the image you created and do something concrete that counters the short-lived feeling.

The concept of self-discipline is also a lasting idea because whatever you want to get rid of needs to stay out for a long time. From pornographic addiction to weight loss, procrastination, etc. - once you overcome these issues, you wouldn't want to go back to the experience again.

Set goals that go beyond what you can enjoy today; remember that long-term achievements are always inspiring even to yourself. You will look back years later and be grateful for the sacrifices you made in the past.

Self-discipline is refined over time and strengthened to resist even bigger temptation but if you start now, if you begin the process of building long term experience, you will become a disciplined person.

Weight loss will be just one of your several achievements because self-discipline for long-term dreams helps you accomplish other things as well. The reason some people might not sustain the long-term approach because they do what is "Easy" instead of doing what is "Right".

Do What's Right, Not What's Easy

The Cure to Laziness (This Could Change Your Life)

There is a thin line between what is right and what is easy such that some people don't know the difference between both concepts. If you pay close attention to your weight loss journey, you will get to know what is right and what is easy making it easier for you to make the right decisions.

Here's a scenario that explains the concept of right and easy: eating just about any food is natural, you can pick up anything from anywhere and eat, this is easy.

What is right on the other hand is to deliberately watch what you eat because eating anything from anywhere is indeed not healthy for your body.

The easy things are always fun, they make you feel free, but you are giving up your freedom without knowing it. Many people do what is easy, they are comfortable with it and wouldn't want to consider anything else.

So, if everyone around you is doing what is easy instead of what is right, change the course of your activities. The most natural things don't take a lot of mental exercises; they are like reflexes, you do them and guess what, they give you zero results. You should do things that align with your goals, in fact, this is how you know what you're doing is right; it takes you closer to your goal.

Your dreams will become a reality when you always do the right things, not the easy ones. The right stuff strengthens your resolve to win; they help you appreciate the weight loss process.

You can "Plan" to do the right things; you can create a schedule that makes you stick to the right events especially when the temptation to slip into easy activities abounds around you.

Learn to stick to the proper routines, create an atmosphere of possibilities around you that limits your choices to only the right ones. If it is so easy for you to avoid the gym so, bring the gym to your home; purchase the equipment and set them in your bedroom. As you wake up in the morning, you don't get to take the easy route; you start the right activity by taking on the gym equipment.

What are those natural things you do that contradict the positive efforts you make? What kind of activities comes naturally to you but aren't healthy? Identify those easy problems and be disciplined enough to kick them out.

Have A PLAN

Creating a plan works with everything! If you are going to get positive results with anything, first create a plan. Especially now that you are on the journey to weight loss, you've got to plan how to eat, what to eat or drink, how to exercise and the things to avoid.

The Cure to Laziness (This Could Change Your Life)

Self-discipline can also be attained when you have a plan; if you stick to what you create, you will get the desired result. Now with this concept, you have got to be very practical and hands-on with the process.

There are a lot of mobile apps that are designed to help people plan for weight loss and some of these apps also make it possible for you to be accountable every day.

If you want to use a manual diary, you must first create the plan (daily or weekly) and create a column for "Daily comments" where you fill out what you did in comparison with what you were supposed to do.

So, at the end of every day, you were using your planner, you can ascertain the areas where you perform excellently as well as the aspects you can work on.

It takes a lot of discipline to stick to a plan, yes, a lot of people know the importance of planning but how many make it work? So, you will be winning on all fronts with this tip; you get to lose weight, become self-disciplined and create a better pattern that adds value to your life.

Planning also makes you do things deliberately so if you want to be intentional about what you do, if you're going to be self-disciplined without feeling so pressured, if you're going to lose some pounds, you need to start to making PLANS towards these goals today.

The desire to lose weight can be more than a wish, and it can come to fruition when you put in the work and do what is required of you. This chapter has shown you how possible it is to set weight loss goals and attain them using the right principles.

For you to achieve anything in life, you must attain some level of discipline and then gradually build on it until you become consistent with it. With weight loss, you can start by being disciplined enough to eat in portions, but you shouldn't remain at this level for too long.

Progressively work towards going beyond just eating in portions by getting off an unhealthy diet entirely instead of just taking them in servings. You may start by taking a walk around your house, improve on that by running, jogging and even getting a gym membership.

As you gradually build on self-discipline, you will be able to stretch your habits, create new plans and stick to purposeful living. If you try to do it all at once, you will not get as many results as you would when you follow a process.

Some of the notions shared in this book are still plans, they are concepts with the excellent potential to work for you if you make them a part-habit. Be committed to the programs and they will become habits, enjoy the patterns and they will lead you to your dreams.

As you implement the suggestions, remember that weight loss isn't the goal; being fit and healthy is the objective. After shedding some

The Cure to Laziness (This Could Change Your Life)

pounds, some fall back to the same unhealthy routines and eating lifestyle, making the entire process unfruitful.

If you are going to enjoy the best of being self-disciplined, you must consider the long-term plan. There are sustainable, long-lasting disciplined habits you can incorporate daily that will make a difference with you on this journey. Flip over to continue your lessons.

Chapter 9:
Long-Term Self-Disciplined Habits

"One Painful Duty Fulfilled Makes the Next Plainer and Easier." - Helen Keller

Self-discipline is a long-term project that entails consistently building up certain habits which make it easier for you to take charge of your life. From the information you've gathered in previous chapters, you understand the crucial role that habits play in helping individuals become self-disciplined.

However, habits must become like a second skin to individuals for sustainable results. It isn't enough to imbibe the habits "Until" you become a disciplined person, you've got to incorporate the practices into every area of life by infusing them into your daily routine.

If the concept of habits for self-discipline is fully integrated, you are bound to make a lot of progress with your life goals.

You don't have to read more about how essential habits are so, just read on as you discover the most results-driven habits that can change your narrative for long-term impact.

The Cure to Laziness (This Could Change Your Life)

You will observe that some of the habits shared in this chapter are straightforward ideas and concepts anyone can implement, which means that attaining self-discipline isn't a complicated process.

More so, the impact habits have on your life isn't determined by the simplicity or complexity of the pattern. By doing what is required of you, permanent changes can start to take place in your life.

Developing a goal-setting habit gives you something worth fighting for such that even in the face of challenges, you are steadfast towards achieving your set goals.

Define A Goal Worth Fighting For

Creating habits without having a definite purpose in mind will cause you to be unstable. First, define a goal you want to achieve, it must be a goal that adds value to your experience when it is completed.

Think about something you've always wanted to do and then set it in your heart as a goal. Next, the goal needs to be deconstructed; this entails breaking down all the pieces of the purpose so you can deal with one piece at a time. If your goals are to lose weight, for example, you've got to break down the essential parts of the goal into the steps you will need to take to accomplish your desired pressure.

As you deconstruct the goal, remember to attach an action plan for each piece, something you can do every day that brings you closer to the goal. Now your responsibility is to ensure that you stick to these action plans one day at a time.

Try not to skip any activity or meal plan that will help you achieve your goal and be committed to doing this for the long haul. This is an example of a lasting habit that encourages self-discipline in a person.

Prioritize the Goal

Before anything else, make sure your goals are prioritized; whatever you do every day should be inspired by the visualization of your objectives. When something becomes top priority, you make it work regardless of the challenges you are faced with.

Rank your goals in order of importance; whatever is most important to you should get all the attention at first. On the other hand, depending on what the actual goal is, you can start with smaller goals; as you succeed with these smaller ones, you will be motivated to take on the bigger goals.

When working with goals, timing is everything. Organize your goals around specific times, so you have deadlines to work with. Do you want to lose weight? How many pounds should go in six months?

After dealing with the smaller goals, you can focus on the top priorities. Devote time from your daily routines to do make the dream a reality; every little step you take matters.

The Cure to Laziness (This Could Change Your Life)

When you start to focus on your prioritized goals and follow your plan religiously, you will be building a habit of consistency that helps you become a disciplined person.

Find Role Models Who Inspire You

Sometimes achieving a goal can be more comfortable when you have role models that encourage you daily. There are people who have walked a similar path like you now and those who have experienced the same trials and won.

You must seek out such individuals because they are the role models that will inspire you to strive for success even in the face of daunting challenges continually. Whenever you want to be so hard on yourself, remember that these role models stumbled some time, but they picked themselves up and moved on.

People who have survived the worse of what you are going through right now are all around you, reach out to them, make a connection and learn from their stories. Some of them might not be in your country, and maybe online via social media.

What are you waiting for? Join them on social media, subscribe to their newsletters, listen to their podcasts, watch their YouTube videos, etc. As you listen, read or watch their content, you will find answers to some Of the issues you deal with and use the answers to strengthen your new habits. While applying the solutions they proffer, you will be building up self-confidence as well.

If the role models you seek are within your immediate environment, you should reach out. Politely ask for a meeting and share your experience while taking note of the suggestions, life lessons and ideas the role model shares with you.

Failure: Even for A Day, Is an Option

The fact that you are creating long-term habits for a self-disciplined life doesn't mean you are immune to failure. Yes, you want to win at all cost, and you are determined to make it work but come on, humans are bound to make mistakes and fail.

It isn't the failure that counts; it's how you respond to it and what you make of it that matters. If you create a plan to perfect a habit for a month and you don't keep up with the idea for a day, it is okay.

Wake Up the Following Day and Make It Work!

Failure is also a learning process; you've got to embrace it and own up to it. Your milestones may not come full circle all the time, but it doesn't mean you aren't making progress. Be open to anything that happens during the process even if it is a mistake.

Keep Track of Your Progress

Failure or not, you are making progress, and you must keep track of it. Having a plan is different from sticking to it; so, by keeping track of your progress, you will be making sure that you follow up with your project.

The Cure to Laziness (This Could Change Your Life)

Get to know how far you've come with your new habits, the areas you need to work on and how you can add some value to the process going forward. If you are not keeping tabs on your progress, you will be unstable with the plans you set up.

When you went to school, you had to write a lot of tests and examinations because the teacher wanted to know if you understood all you've been taught. Without those tests and exams, you wouldn't have made it to the next level of your education.

So, do you see why progress reports are critical? They help you monitor all you do and keep you in check. Keeping track of your progress also creates an opportunity for improvement in areas you haven't performed well.

As you keep track, you also discover the differences between what you are doing right now and what you are "Supposed" to do. The former is always convenient but may not be the right thing while the latter is what gets you the desired results.

Set Monthly Milestones

Setting a monthly benchmark is a habit everyone should incorporate. Having goals is a good thing but having landmarks that help you stick to your goals is even better.

If you want a long-term goal that may take up to six months, you will need monthly milestones that keep you focused throughout the period you try to attain the goal. Split the goal into monthly achievements, work towards making sure the monthly sub-goals are met and assess your progress at the month's end. Sometimes your goals may be too big for you, in fact, you might feel overwhelmed by them, and this is normal.

But by cultivating the habit of breaking down goals into monthly milestones, you will be able to handle your aspirations in the most confident and timely manner yet. Using milestones also help you become a disciplined person who is conscious of the fact that there must be a monthly progress report at the end of the month.

So, you strive to do the needful every month until the completion of the goal. Milestones also keep you focused, fully engaged and committed to your goals.

Self-Analyze Your Progress

As you take steps toward your goals every day, you need to pause at some point to analyze your progress. Getting to know how far you have come will help you determine what you can do to become even better.

Some people become consumed with the idea of making progress that they don't even know when they aren't attuned to the plan anymore. It is okay to take a break and observe some moments of self-introspection, these moments help you appreciate the progress you've made and serves as an opportunity for you to make plans concerning the areas that aren't perfect.

Monitoring your progress is an avenue for you to observe the patterns that work for you and the ones that don't. If you have been doing things the wrong way, you will discover why and then you can also strengthen the effort you put into making your goals become a reality.

If you made time to plan, then you will have the material that will serve as a reference point for you to analyze your progress. Check your plans; match the ones you wrote to the ones you achieved and find out why others weren't realized.

At the end of your self-analysis, you will experience increased motivation to take on better habits and do more towards achieving your goals.

Remove Negative Habits

While analyzing your progress, take the time to obliterate negative habits. You are trying to instill the right habits that will help you become a disciplined person, but you will not achieve the proper habits when you still got the negative ones hovering all around you.

At this stage, everything you do should be in sync with the new habits you are trying to formulate. You know the habits you struggle with; you know the activities that cause you to take steps backward in your quest to be disciplined.

Well, go beyond identifying bad habits and start getting rid of them. The old habits will not make your transition process easier nor will they help you achieve your goals. Those negative habits you are struggling with can make an early exit at this stage because you are implementing a lot of changes with your habits now. However, don't expect the bad habits to disappear; you've got to work towards it making this a reality.

For every bad habit you want to remove, prepare to replace it with a good practice that becomes a part of your new goal plan. Show how disciplined you can be by kicking out unproductive habits and retaining the good habits that inspire you to become better.

Keep Pushing For 30 Days Straight

If you can keep up with a pattern for as long as 30 days, you can be sure that you have gained the mastery over it. The habits and ideas shared in this chapter will only become impactful when you are committed to doing them regularly.

Having the 30-day goal in mind helps you maintain focus; you wake up daily knowing that you've got fewer days left and time is running out. When you create your "Goal plan" make sure it cuts across 30 days.

Within the plan, have sections that contain action plans for the first five, fifteen and twenty-five days. By the time you get to the twenty-ninth day, you should be able to have a progress report.

The Cure to Laziness (This Could Change Your Life)

Following a 30-day plan is a recipe for long-term discipline you will be building yourself to achieve your goals at the same time. When creating your unique 30-day plan, the first seven days should be about simpler tasks that help you ease into the habit. After these first seven days, take things up a notch by the second week and continue to raise the bar until the last day.

By the thirtieth day, if you were strict with adhering to the plan, you will have amazing results to show for the hard work, dedication and commitment. Life can be very easy, fun-filled and inspiring if you create a system that works. Through your habits, it is possible to live your best life today as you fight off negative experiences that are enhanced by being undisciplined.

For some people, they enjoy the benefits of having the right habits for only a short period and in that amount of time, they attest to the impact it has over their lives. The reason such person relapses and become undisciplined again is that they didn't build up sustainable, long-term habits.

The information shared with you in this section repositions you for success in life. The addictions and problems you struggled with in the past will no longer hold you down because you've consolidated your habits with your daily routines.

The initial challenge with building long-term habits is keeping up with the pattern every day, therefore the 30-day milestone must be taken seriously. If you can sustain the same process for 30 days, then you've got it for life! Work towards achieving the 30-day plan and watch your habits become increasingly progressive such that being disciplined isn't a struggle anymore.

Chapter 10:
The 3 Proven Methods

"I used to walk down the street like I was a superstar… I want people to walk around delusional about how great they can be – and then to fight so hard for it every day that the lie becomes the truth."
- Lady Gaga

Some ideas are so simple to handle when thinking about self-discipline, you need to apply them to your peculiar experience and watch them work. However, most of these "Simple" steps aren't always adequately harnessed, they can be overlooked for the more complex ones, and this must change.

This chapter introduces you to three powerful yet straightforward methods that will transform your life in the most amazing ways possible. They are the three proven techniques that will shape you into the man or woman you want to be.

But the idea behind having "Tips" and "Steps" shouldn't deter you from creating more out of the box ideas that work for you. For instance, you may want to utilize these techniques for a specific challenge, but that doesn't mean you can't use them for something else.

Every idea, suggestion, concept, or plan you have read through in this book can change your life's narrative completely in more ways than one.

So, while keeping your eyes on the specific goal you've got for your life, remember that you can cause a change with other areas of your life, but first do you know who are?

Know Your Identity

It is easy to assume; you know who you are, after all, you have been living your life for so many years now right? Well, this assumption is always erroneous because there are still a lot of people who do not have a firm grasp of their identity.

Knowing who you are is crucial to achieving your long-term goals. When you are self-aware, you tend to do things that are in sync with your dreams. Your journey to being self-disciplined will be a successful one based on how well you know yourself.

You wouldn't want to quit habits because other people are doing it, neither will you want to establish new patterns for others. Everything you do will be inspired by your desire to fill the gaps in your life because you know who you are now.

The Cure to Laziness (This Could Change Your Life)

When you know who you are, it also becomes increasingly comfortable for you to shift your thoughts such that you don't go back to the wrong things.

If you are dealing with laziness and a desire to be fit, a discovery of who you are will propel you to take strategic steps towards curtailing laziness.

More so, you will think and believe that you are not a lazy person because that is what self-discovery does. Your words and actions will be tailored towards fighting off laziness because unlike in the past, you are empowered with information and greater knowledge about yourself.

How Can You Start on The Path to Self-Discovery?

Firstly, what are your values? What are those things you hold dear to you? The ideas you know you will never compromise your values, and values are motivating factors that keep you going even when you are down and out. Take some time to discover your values and align them with your long-term goals.

Another way to know your identity is through your interests; these are your passions, hobbies or anything that draws your attention. The things you are curious and concerned about constitute your interests. This idea is so important because when you know the things that interest you, they take you closer to your goals.

Of course, your temperament also matters when knowing your identity. Some people struggle with being self-disciplined because they don't know their character. You've got to see if you are a people's person, an introvert, extrovert, an organizer, etc.

Think about this for a moment; a person is trying to lose weight, he/she has been going to the gym and other fitness places with many people but hasn't made any real progress. After each session at the gym, the person feels like it was all a waste of time and cannot wait to get out of the crowd.

Over time, this person stops going to the gym and forgets about the weight loss goal. Well, the problem here is that the person hasn't discovered his/her identity through the temperament.

It is possible that this individual is an introvert and tends to learn faster alone. By continually going to the gym where there are a lot of people, the individual will not achieve his/her goals.

On the brighter side, if this person takes the time to discover his/her identity, to know who he is and embraces it, fitness sessions can take place at home with sustainable and long-term results.

You can discover your identity by getting to know your strengths and weaknesses, we all have areas of greatness and some flaws. Identifying the fields, you are extremely good at will help you achieve a whole lot within a short time as opposed to doing things you aren't so good at and not making anything.

Be honest with your assessment of self in discovering your strengths and weaknesses; this idea will be constructive when you try to take steps towards achieving your goals. However, life is continually evolving, and you change periodically, the areas of weakness can become stronger points for you and vice versa. The key to knowing your identity and utilizing the information for self-discipline is so you can stay true to yourself.

Don't be something you are not, embrace every aspect of your life as you strive to become better daily. Spend time with yourself, ask questions, observe your decision-making process and you will get to know your identity. But it doesn't end with knowing who you are; there are other concepts you must also consider for long-term results as a disciplined individual.

Use Reward and Punishment

Now that you know who you are, you will be more inclined to start doing the right things that inspire you on this journey to self-discipline. But there is a challenge with doing the right thing; some people do not take the right steps seriously despite the knowledge that these steps will add value to them.

So, it is possible for a person to know that drinking a lot of water is healthy and not try to drink because he/she doesn't want to. This attitude breeds incompetence and laziness; it also makes it difficult for anyone to make progress with an idea.

It is not cool for you to self-sabotage your journey. You know why you want to be a disciplined person so why aren't you doing what is required? Why do you deliberately ignore the process because there are no consequences?

Until you start to utilize the concept of punishment and rewards, you may struggle for a long time with your aspirations despite knowing what to do.

Everything you have read from the introductory section until now has prepared you for a self-disciplined life, so you have the tools and ideas you should implement. If you set up a daily, weekly or monthly plan, be mindful of how you execute your programs.

If you carry out your plans for a period, then reward yourself for a job well done. Your reward can be something that also reinforces the bigger idea you are trying to accomplish or something that motivates you to become better.

You shouldn't wait until you accomplish something grand before rewarding yourself. If you start with a milestone, upon completion reward yourself, it might be a high-five, some words of kindness to yourself or a tap on your back.

The Cure to Laziness (This Could Change Your Life)

When you attain a more significant milestone, do something you've always wanted to do for yourself, something that motivates you such that you can do much more about achieving your goals. Rewards are excellent concepts that give you a significant boost, they make you believe in yourself, and this is a major propelling factor for anyone who wants to achieve success in life.

There is a flip side to gaining rewards, and it is punishment. Just as you are quick to reward yourself when you do the right things, be swift with punishment when you don't. You don't need an accountability partner to tell you when you should be punished, what you need is to be stern with yourself.

How important is the goal you want to achieve? If it is essential, then you should be prepared to punish yourself for not sticking to the processes that will make you attain the goal. Instead of giving yourself something you always dreamed about as you did with benefits, you should withdraw some privileges.

Sometimes, you may have to resort to high negative punishments that cause you to realize how far you have derailed from the goal. The activities you enjoy should be cut short so you can focus on the bigger picture.

The times of punishment will also serve as a reminder that your commitment to excellence cannot be compromised. After several punishments and deprivations, you will be strategically positioning yourself for more productive ventures that will bring you closer to your dreams.

You should strike a balance between reward and punishment, if you are going to be extreme with one, do the same for the other. Being overtly radical with discipline and not doing the same for rewards can lead to discouragement.

For you to avoid being discouraged, you might want to maintain a balanced approach to both ideals such that there is room for second chances and opportunities to try again till you perfect the process.

If you continue with this pattern, you will arrive at a level where you don't have to punish yourself to get things done. You do the right things every day because you have programmed your mind to stick to the steps that guarantee success. At the end of the day, because of the reward/punishment process, you will be empowering yourself to shatter glass ceilings and become an inspiration to others.

Set Yourself Up for Success

One of the products of the reward/punishment system is that it sets you up for success. By following through with the things, you need to do to avoid punishment and gain rewards; you will be motivated to them without such consequences.

By setting yourself up for success, you will be able to take steps towards your dreams without being prompted to; it all just happens

The Cure to Laziness (This Could Change Your Life)

naturally. This level of success doesn't occur spontaneously, it takes time to build and maintain, but it is always worth it in the end.

Success is an idea; it is never finite. You must continually press forward to make it happen, but the process to embracing that idea requires a lot of work, and this entails you doing what should be done regardless of your moods, feelings or affiliations at the time.

You must plan your future today by telling those stiff challenges to crumble before you by taking decisive actions towards your goals. You have the first steps already by learning about yourself and knowing what you want out of life, but it doesn't stop at knowing.

Devote your time and energy to those goals that are meaningful, we are talking about strategy here. Setting up for success means you are aware of what you want and then you are creating a strategy towards accomplishing it.

Decide to move onwards and say, "I don't want to know how hard this is, I am not letting go until I get the best out of this situation". By saying the most inspiring words to yourself, more effort is required, and it can be achieved by utilizing one word: FOCUS!

At this stage, you transcend the feeling of seeking rewards or averting punishment; you are convinced of the potency of the process that you find yourself doing them daily by being focused.

Focus means setting your sights on the results even before kickstarting the process; it means doing what is required and moving beyond mistakes or future worries. Focus helps you become an exceptional person who isn't seeking perfection but making continuous effort towards one goal. You will be confident in your strengths and self-worth knowing that you can fix any problem.

You must learn how to set yourself up for success by taking charge of your life and make the necessary changes when required. Create realistic strategies and stick to them even in difficult times.

Dreams will never become real until you intentionally set yourself for success. If you converse with someone who has achieved remarkable things, you will observe that they did two things effectively; they set goals and created a pathway that connects them to the targets.

Now, these successful people stick to that pathway regardless of what happens, they have big dreams and do not set limits. Don't listen to great people and forget to implement what you learn; their stories should serve as a springboard for your dreams.

Tell yourself that if they did it, you could do it also. Remember to become passionate about what you believe in; sometimes passion is what keeps you focused; passion will always help you get to your destination.

The Cure to Laziness (This Could Change Your Life)

The process of setting yourself up for success requires a lot of discipline, but when you succeed with it and start implementation, you will become self-disciplined and self-motivated.

While anticipating the results of your goals, live in the reality of it happening; you will be setting yourself up for success when you do. In addition to all you've learned in this book, make good use of these three proven methods. When you know who you are, it becomes easy to set yourself up for success while taking measures to discipline yourself when you fall short of expectations.

Think about the area of life where you need more motivation; how can these methods help you improve? When you take the lessons gained and make them a part of your life, it becomes easy for you to experience changes and positive results.

After you get the results you desire from the challenges you want to change, continue to apply these techniques for a more robust experience. Self-discipline isn't attained when you no longer suffer from the addiction or the issues you battle with.

You don't get the assurance of discipline because you have lost weight; you achieve it by surpassing your goals. Self-discipline is a product of continuous efforts, application of techniques and steps taken to uplift oneself daily. The idea that one step makes you attain discipline is often misleading, so use these three methods provided in this section to change the narrative of your experience.

Changing the narrative also means taking control of your life and living on your terms. It means acknowledging the fact that there may be issues to deal with, but you are ready to stick to your beliefs and succeed. More information about how you can take charge of your life is in the next section.

Chapter 11:
Taking Control of your Life

"The ability to subordinate an impulse to a value is the essence of the proactive person." - Stephen Covey

A person doesn't become self-disciplined without being in control. The concept of gaining control over one's life must be embraced and practiced by everyone because it is a necessary factor for success with discipline. Everything you have read in this book was intentionally put together to help YOU. It doesn't matter if you share this experience with someone else, that person cannot use the information for your good.

So, this means that you must oversee your narrative, be aware that you are the only one who is going to affect a change in your life and that is what it means to take control. Before deliberating more about taking control, you should know that a conversation around taking back control could signify that a person has lost control previously.

Control over one's life is not always lost to another person; sometimes people lose control of themselves to an idea, their environment, or a vague concept that takes them off the disciplined path.

Regardless of what you relinquished control for, you must regain it now because it is required for the journey of self-discipline. Taking control of your life starts with the process of rediscovering what motivates you, learning how to take care of yourself, doing the things you love and making time for the people you care about. How are you going to do that?

Practice Having "Me" Time

From the beginning of the week until the last day of the month, some people are occupied with work, meetings and every other activity other than creating time for themselves.

They are always on the move, thinking about the next deal or idea to execute and even when they have some time that should be used for themselves, they look for something else to keep them busy.

To take control of your life, it is crucial that you have some "Me" time because it offers you an opportunity to stay in touch with your goals and aspirations while disconnecting from activities that clog your time.

The "Me" times you create, will give you a significant positive boost and energy required for the bigger goals you want to attain. If you cannot control your time, then it will be impossible for you to control your life.

Start taking charge of your life by first taking control of your time. Regardless of your obligations, "Me" time is essential and the more you implement it, the better your chances of taking control of your life. As you create time for yourself, you will also want to try new things.

Try New Things

This is one habit you will be grateful you developed. People who do not have control over their lives cannot try new things. They are always held down by the expectations of others or by other things they think they should be doing.

If you feel like your life is being run by activities and you aren't the one in charge, change the situation by trying new things you ordinarily wouldn't decide on your own. Break free from the constraints of sticking to familiar routines and events you are used to, come on! Life is all about being daring, and it does take a certain level of discipline to try new ventures.

You may not have to try new things every single day but do try them periodically. Step away from your comfort zone, live freely and enjoy every moment. What you will observe as you try this step is that you will be in better control of your life, you will be able to do the things you want to do while staying happy with yourself.

Let's talk about happiness for a moment, shall we? When a person is in control of his/her life, the feeling of happiness is constant. You will always be satisfied with your life such that there are no insecurities nor internal problems.

What are the things you have always wanted to try out? Skydiving? Are you taking a trip to Africa? Or babysitting? Volunteering? Whatever you want to do, take control of your life and time.

As you build yourself up on this path to self-discipline, be comfortable with the idea of breaking the rules sometimes. Everyone will tell you to do the same thing repeatedly, but it is okay to get a breather and do something new.

Make this the year of saying "Yes" to new and positive adventures while exploring a wide range of options. Build up your experience bank with new memories, and you may ask "What if my love for trying out new things affects my plan for self-discipline?"

The answer to that question is encapsulated in one word: planning. The idea for you to try new things isn't to make you undisciplined. With careful consideration and planning, you can fit your entire schedule (including the new ideas) into your routine and make it work.

You will be able to handle everything you should be doing when you dedicate time to planning. However, open your heart to continuous learning through new things. Experiences gained by exploration of new ideas will always be of immense benefit to you.

As you try new things, something remarkable happens to you as well which also helps you take better control of your life. You will observe that you have become kinder to yourself which is one of the hallmarks of a disciplined person.

Treat Yourself Well as You Would Others

We are always quick to express kindness to others, society raises us to say the right things, to reach out to someone else and make them smile but what about being kind to self?

Some people who have tried being proactive about new things attest to the fact that it made them very kind to themselves. They no longer held themselves back from enjoying a treat or getting themselves a present because they are starting to be adventurous.

Well, a significant way for you to take charge of your life is to treat yourself the way you would treat others (positively of course). When you are deliberate about being kind to yourself, you will be taking control of what happens to you.

It is okay to expect kindness from other people especially when you are also kind as well, but when you feel bad because other people aren't helpful to you, you unknowingly give them control of your life.

This is the year it ends; this is the season to take back control of your life and not allow anyone to get the best of your emotions. If there are certain dishes you only use to serve your guests, get them out and use them for your meal.

Say kind words to yourself every day, get yourself flowers and do all those nice things you would do for other people. Remember that you are on this pathway that promises great results, so you've got nothing to lose.

When other people do something, they're not proud of, they look to you for kind words, and you try to make them feel alright. But if you make a mistake on this journey to self-discipline, you become so hard on yourself. So, it seems like you set the bar too high for yourself and don't do the same for the people around you.

Give yourself a break by treating yourself with the same kind of respect you have for others and continually tell yourself you deserve the best. Now you are wondering how this connects to your self-discipline journey.

Well, only people who take control of their lives excel with self-discipline; treating yourself with kindness as you will treat others is an opportunity to oversee your life, and that helps you become a disciplined person.

Enjoy the Power of Saying "NO."

The Cure to Laziness (This Could Change Your Life)

If you say "Yes" to all requests from everyone who asks, you will be losing control of your life. There is so much power in saying no because it helps you take back control. People don't want to say "No" because they don't want to feel guilty or hurt someone else, but can you make the entire world happy? If you always put the satisfaction of other people ahead of what you want, you will NOT be a self-disciplined person.

For example, if you decide to lose weight today, you might have to stay off some food or activities for a while. As you try to get rid of these items that make you struggle with weight loss, your friends may want to continue in the same unhealthy pattern.

So, they invite you over for parties where unhealthy foods are served, they don't want to exercise, they encourage your bad eating habits, and because you don't want them to feel bad or you don't want to be the boring one in the group, you give in to their suggestions every time.

The more you say "Yes" to them, the more control they assert over your life. Gradually, you will not remember your goals to lose weight, you will not be inspired to do the things that must be done, and you will no longer be motivated to do anything that makes you self-disciplined.

Control over your life is determined by the number of "No's" you say to requests that do not add value to your experience. You mustn't be a part of every event that takes place; selectivity is a trait disciplined people exhibit.

Realize that you own your time and only say yes to what adds value to it. The urge to please everyone stems from an undisciplined mindset; it is the fastest way to pulling down everything you've learned so don't allow it even for a moment.

Now self-discipline also comes to play here in another form; some people can say "No," but they cannot sustain it. So, they say "No," but if the person who is asking probes further with continuous requests and pleas, they say "Yes." This trait is referred to as being indecisive.

Indecisive people do not become disciplined; they struggle with the idea of pleasing themselves and other people that they become conflicted. Don't be an indecisive person! Be bold to make decisions and stick by them; by doing this, you will be taking control of your life and building up self-discipline as well.

What Is Life Teaching You?
Life is filled with lessons; if you are observant enough, you will never stop learning. Take control of your life by learning life-long lessons through the activities and events you experience daily.

We often try to resist life's lessons because they come in ways we don't expect, some lessons are in the form of mistakes, and because

The Cure to Laziness (This Could Change Your Life)

we are so consumed with the idea of being perfect, we miss the lesson embedded in the experience.

Embrace all that life teaches you, and you will know how to gain control over your own life. If you had a challenging experience, don't focus on the challenge itself or how it affects you. Try to figure out what you can learn from the problem.

The next time you are faced with a similar challenge, you will be able to handle it better because of the lesson you learned from the previous experience. However, this time you've gained control over your life; you will not be uncomfortable with the issue or distraught because life's lesson has strengthened you.

So, ask yourself right now; what is life teaching you? From everything that has happened to you, what have you learned? How have the experiences made you better? You will know when you are in control of life when experiences do not define your mood or attitude towards self-discipline.

With lessons from life, you can create an atmosphere of wisdom around you such that you always know what to do every time you are faced with a situation, and this is what being in control of one's life means.

A problem can pave the way for multiple solutions in your life, pay attention to what experiences are teaching you; you will be amazed at how far you grow into becoming a self-disciplined person who inspires others to take the same path.

A person who has gained control over his/her life will enjoy the benefits of self-discipline. Power makes independence possible; it helps you do what you want to do when you should do it and encourages you to continue the path you have created for yourself.

You become aware of the power you possess to cause changes and rely on your strength for positive results. The absence of control makes you susceptible to irregular activities; today you feel excited about self-discipline by doing the right things, and the following day, you are not so enthusiastic.

Unbalanced decisions do not blend with discipline, but you can correct this pattern by being in charge. It's okay to take suggestions and advice, but if the people around you are not giving you the best advice, then it is time to take control of your life.

- Do the things you want to do.

- Trust the process you create.

- Believe in your ability to win.

The above progressions are just some of the ways you can take control of your life. Tell yourself these truths every day, and you will be able to combat the feeling of losing control. Your life can be fun,

The Cure to Laziness (This Could Change Your Life)

progressive and inspiring; what you need to do is TAKE CHARGE! Own your truth and don't stop building yourself on the path to self-discipline.

Conclusion

Self-discipline is an attainable virtue anyone can imbibe especially when the individual has a manual to follow. There is a process for everything that can be achieved in life and what you have received from this book is a definitive guide containing the significant aspects you can work on consistently until you reach your desired goal.

The fact that you are reading a book on self-discipline shows how committed you are to the process but is process enough? Can a person become self-disciplined just by sticking to a method?

It's akin to having a reading timetable for an upcoming examination. While having a schedule is brilliant, does having it alone guarantee a pass at the exam? As mentioned in a previous chapter, being process-oriented isn't enough, you've got to go beyond adopting the process and be more conscious of the protocol it entails.

By protocol, we mean the rules of conduct and behavior to imbibe for a wish to become a reality. Without a procedure, the process will not be enough. As you implement everything you've learned with this material, remember that the purpose of it all is to help you establish a protocol that makes the process a part of your daily reality.

The Cure to Laziness (This Could Change Your Life)

So, with forming new habits, for example, you shouldn't be fixated on just "How" to create the pattern. You should however become more conscious about the activities you can do every day that will strengthen the newly formulated habit.

Your ability to maintain the lessons learned in the sections of this book will determine how impactful your experience will be. This will ultimately introduce the concept of sustainability in life.

The internet is replete with information about how everyone can become better with self-discipline yet, millions of people still struggle with the idea of taking charge of their own lives. One can only wonder why this is a case, with so much knowledge out there.

Well, the reason for the above assertion is a lack of sustaining power; too many people read, but only a few implements what they discover. For you to create a connection between theories and results, you must become passionate about sustainability.

Having good habits, building a positive mindset, taking control of your life and every other idea you gleaned from this book can become a vital part of your life long-term if you are deliberate about sustaining them.

This means you are going to apply the concepts every day (regardless of how the results trickle in). And while using them, remember that the process is just a means to an end, what matters the most is the pattern you establish which is also known as the "Protocol".

Nothing can successfully stand in the way of a person who is determined to become self-disciplined. Through this book, you have gained access to applicable patterns that will provide useful results that take you from where you are now to where you want to be. What are you waiting for to get started?

Mental Toughness and True Grit

Develop an Unbeatable Mindset, the Self-Discipline to Succeed, achieve a Champion's Mind, the Willpower of a Navy Seal, and Become an Elite Spartan with Self-Control

Introduction

Quite often, when we see successful people, we imagine that they had help in achieving their success. We assume that they came from a rich family or that they were afforded more opportunities than the average person. While this may be true in some instances, the truth of the matter is that what makes most people successful isn't their family or their luck. Rather, most people achieve success with the help of mental toughness and self-discipline. These attributes enable a person to apply themselves with greater effect, thereby giving them a better chance of successfully realizing their dreams.

This book will explore the concepts of mental toughness and self-discipline, explaining their various forms and techniques. In the end, you will know enough about these qualities to be able to apply them to your life, thus giving you the tools, you need to achieve your goals and realize your dreams!

The secret behind the story of every successful person in the world is self-discipline. No goals, achievement, or even personal success is ever achieved without self-discipline. It is remarkably an essential trait any person needs to possess in order to accomplish excellence. Whether you are aiming for success in your personal or professional life, everything starts with the power to control your behavior, desires, and emotions through discipline. Self-discipline is having the ability to refuse instant pleasure and gratification in favor of long-term fulfillment and satisfaction from attaining bigger and more significant goals.

It's important to understand how to direct yourself to accomplish your goals. Discipline is the primary ingredient in the recipe of success. Self-discipline isn't something new. Humanity has known of its virtues since the days of antiquity, or it wouldn't have made the wondrous progress it has made down the millennia. From building the magnificent pyramids more than five thousand years ago and the invention of the first automobile to putting a man on the moon and today's smartphones and computers, none of humanity's marvelous achievements would have been possible without self-disciple. We would still be savages living in caves, interested only in eating, sleeping, and mating.

Is it any surprise then that, for years and years, it has been a subject of discussion and something that defined the most successful people in the world? One of the most creative writers in history stated, "Self-discipline is the ability to do what you should do when you should do it, whether you feel like it or not." Successful people know that it's the way to any achievements in life. They mastered the technique of self-discipline to help them to succeed. They managed to include the habit of self-discipline in conjunction with a series of virtuous habits. This, in turn, certainly helped them see things more clearly and become the success they were. If they were able to do it, you can as well.

Self-discipline will help you make the right decisions, take necessary action, and carry out your plan no matter how many difficulties or hindrances it brings as you travel along your chosen path.

Being disciplined doesn't necessarily mean that you must limit yourself or set restrictions in your lifestyle. You don't need to give up the things that you enjoy doing or let go of the fun, excitement, and relaxation in your life. It would be a big mistake on your part to equate self-discipline with punishment of some sort. You discipline yourself to achieve a larger goal that, in fact, gives you immense happiness.

The essence of self-discipline is learning ways to center your mind and focus your energies on the goals you set and work hard to achieve them. Also, you develop a mindset where your choices lead you rather than your bad habits, emotions, or even what others say. Self-discipline enables you to achieve your goals within a sensible time frame, as well as enjoy a more organized and rewarding life.

Chapter 1:
Mental Toughness

Mental toughness is the ability to keep going even if situations in life are trying to drag you down. Life is not always easy, and unfortunately, sometimes we all must deal with relationship problems, stressful dead-end jobs, or money problems. If you have ever dealt with these types of issues, you might have felt stuck in your situation, unable to see a way out. You might have felt like you would be in the situation forever. If you have ever felt like this, you know it can feel nearly impossible to make a change in your life when you are dealing with that overwhelming "stuck" feeling. That feeling can be very defeating, and it is these situations that either require us to summon our mental toughness and turn our lives around for the better or remain in the situation and feel increasingly more defeated.

Everyone is going to experience hardships throughout their lives, but it is how we deal with these hardships that can really make or break us. Summoning your mental toughness, developing the characteristics of a mentally tough person, and improving your emotional intelligence are all ways in which you can improve your mental toughness and, in turn, your life.

A mentally tough person uses certain psychological factors and tricks to change their mindset, hence improving their entire life around for the better. By setting boundaries, practicing good communication skills, maintaining a schedule, and employing certain methods used by professional athletic coaches and military leaders, you can change your life for the better and eliminate fear and anxiety in your life once and for all.

You will be able to use setbacks you encounter as opportunities—a springboard so to speak that creates a jumping-off point for you to evaluate your life and embrace the changes and challenges you encounter as a growing point instead of a negative setback. Finally, you will be able to rein in your anger, refocusing it for a better purpose and using the energy you experience from the anger as a method to achieve great things.

What's so special about mental toughness? To put it simply, possessing it can raise your thinking processes above the patterns and superficial usage of your brain. It challenges your mind by tapping into higher level thinking processes. The greatest minds as recorded in history, starting from Aristotle to Albert Einstein to Bill Gates and so many more, have all been great critical thinkers. Before you decide that there is no way you could claim to think like these amazing people, please realize that mental toughness has very little to do with intelligence. While great thinkers are often intelligent, they aren't all geniuses. They are set apart by the fact that they trained their minds to think beyond the norm and beyond the limitations so often assumed and accepted by most people. They utilized what they possessed and ensured it becomes more. That is what mental toughness offers you.

Anyone can be a critical thinker. It is a set of skills that can be learned, practiced, and perfected. All the knowledge you need to sharpen your skills and become a strong critical thinker is in the following pages. You must sacrifice your effort and time to achieve the results you want. Just like the great thinkers of the past and present, your mind is capable of limitless possibilities!

Characteristics of Mentally Tough Individuals

Mental toughness is something that everyone can develop, but it does seem as if it comes more easily to some people. Have you ever noticed that some people could face conflicts head-on, sail through adverse situations, and come out better for it in the end? Anyone who can embrace a challenging situation with arms wide open probably has a great level of mental toughness, and you too can acquire this mentality. Most mentally tough people have similar personality characteristics, and these characteristics can all be developed with a little patience and practice. You bought this book because you already know that you want to make a change in your life and recognizing the need to make a change is the first and most important step. You, too, can develop the following characteristics to improve your mental toughness.

Confidence

Confidence is a huge factor in mental toughness. Confident people can remain resilient to change because they know they will come out okay in the end, regardless of what happens. Your mental state contributes a large percentage in whether you succeed or fail. Confident people are more assertive and can take charge of their situation to make the needed changes, hence developing an outcome that works out in their favor. For example, someone who lacks self-confidence might falter when deciding, changing their minds several times or maybe even avoid deciding in the first place. A confident person will decide and stick with it, knowing that they can use obstacles as an opportunity for growth. Confident people charge ahead, making decisions to get things accomplished. They envision an outcome and work toward it. They know that Henry Ford was right when he said, "Whether you think you can or think you can't, you're right."

Ability to Welcome Change and Remain Flexible

A mentally tough person can welcome change and roll with the punches, whether the change is big or small. Change is not necessarily bad, and often, if there is no change in your life, you are not growing as a person. Life is about learning and trying new things and remaining in the same situation does not allow for growth or improvement in your life. A mentally tough person will embrace a challenge and adapt to change, often viewing the change, no matter how big or small, as a chance to develop a new skill or experience a new opportunity. There is the old saying that goes, "The closure of one door results to the opening of another door," and sometimes a forced change is all we need to get us out of the stagnant place in which we are stuck. For example, in today's economy, jobs and businesses are constantly changing and restructuring. When companies downsize or restructure, employees are faced with job loss, and this can sometimes be devastating. A mentally strong person will seize the opportunity to improve their life by weighing all their options. If a mentally strong person who had been considering a career change suddenly lost his or her job, he or she will take this time to develop their skill set, return to school, or polish his or her résumé to make a career change. Maybe that mentally strong person had been considering starting his or her own business but didn't have the time or the knowledge to make it happen. This person will view this sudden abundance of extra time as a chance to grow and develop as a person, starting his or her business and making things happen, instead of lounging in front of the television and crying relentlessly about their situation.

Refuse to Let Fear Hold Them Back

Mentally tough people do not let fear hold them back. Everyone must go through challenges in life, and it is how we view those challenges that can shape our lives for the better. Change is scary, but so is remaining in the same stagnant situation indefinitely. Moving to a new city, completely changing careers, or leaving a relationship can be scary; but the reality is that you are considering this change for a reason. Maybe you're unhappy with the job opportunities in your small town. Maybe there is no room for growth in your current career. Maybe you and your partner have some differences that cannot be resolved with a compromise. Whatever the situation is, mentally strong people do not let fear of the unknown hold them back.

Think about the area in your life in which you want to make a change. Now think about how you would feel if you are in this exact same situation a year, two years, or even five years from now. Will you be even more miserable? Even though change can be terrifying, it is often even more terrifying to remain stuck in the same situation indefinitely, all because you fear the unknown. Mentally tough people would rather be scared for a short amount of time while they are going through a change in life than live in fear of the change, never improving or bettering their situation.

Will Not Let Toxic People Affect Them

A toxic person is someone who ruins the environment or the atmosphere for those around them. A toxic person might be incredibly jealous, judgmental, or just negative overall. A toxic person is like the grown-up version of the playground bully: he or she has low self-esteem and is so unhappy with his or her own life, so they are constantly trying to bring others down to their level. The toxic person might discredit all your ideas or find something that can go wrong in every situation. The toxic person is usually projecting their own insecurities onto you, sometimes unknowingly. The toxic person is not a mentally healthy person and can quickly drag others down. Someone who is mentally strong will avoid this type of person in general, or at the very least, not let the toxic person's opinions bother them.

In some situations, it is impossible to avoid toxic people. If there exists a venomous individual in your workplace, odds are you can't always avoid this person. A mentally strong person realizes this and will do his or her best to see things from the toxic person's point of view if possible. A mentally strong person also realizes that the toxic person is unhappy, so he or she will not let the toxic opinions and attitude affect him or her and his or her work. Although the mentally strong person might not agree with the toxic person's opinion, the mentally strong person will listen to the toxic person's opinion and does not engage in an argument. The mentally strong person has the knowledge and the self-esteem to treat everyone with respect even if they do not agree with what is being said. The mentally strong person knows that the toxic person is just that, toxic, and he or she will not let this person ruin his or her day or the outcome of a situation.

Exert Assertiveness

Mentally strong people are assertive. They say what they mean, and they mean what they say. They know how to use concise language so that the meaning of their words is not mistaken, and their intentions are not taken the wrong way. Mentally strong people know how to say no. They know that it's okay to take time to themselves, whether that means saying no to an invitation they don't want to accept or simply staying in on a Saturday night to recharge. Mentally strong people also know when to set boundaries. For example, if someone asks them a personal question and they don't want to answer the question, the mentally strong person will have no problem saying that they are uncomfortable answering the question. Mentally strong people can stick up for themselves and do not let other people take advantage of them.

The Difference Between Being Mentally Strong and Acting Tough

A person who is "acting tough" is most likely someone who is not mentally strong. The tough person uses intimidation tactics to fake their own mental strength. They might bully other people by taking control of a situation, or they might simply demand that things go their way, never willing to compromise or listen to anyone else's opinion.

Sometimes when working on a task requiring everyone to collaborate and discuss solutions for a mutually agreeable outcome, someone would insist that everything goes his or her way. That person is probably just acting tough and, in all actuality, is insecure. As previously discussed, a mentally strong person can remain flexible in most situations. He or she embraces change and welcomes challenges.

Tough people can put themselves in someone else's shoes to better understand another viewpoint while a tough-acting people live to feel

Mental Toughness and True Grit

powerful. To them, being in charge, running the show, and bossing people around make them feel powerful. Although this toughness may make someone seem invincible at first glance, the tough-acting person only sees one way in which to solve a problem: their way. If their way does not work to solve the said problem or complete a task, the tough-acting person will be devastated. Tough-acting people do not embrace change or view failure as a chance to develop because they do not have the ability to see how their perceived failure can help them grow. Tough-acting people only see one thing: failure. Their ego is damaged, and they are unable to embrace the challenge to learn the lesson of how things can be improved for next time.

A mentally strong person knows there is more than one way to solve a problem. He or she not only welcomes other people's viewpoints but also uses failure as a chance to grow and develop, constantly improving as a person. He or she will take other opinions into consideration and try to see things from all angles.

Chapter 2: Self-Discipline

What Is Willpower?

Willpower can be defined as the ability to set a course of action and work toward it by fully engaging and being proactive. It is your ability to control any harmful or unnecessary impulses. It is the ability to overcome procrastination and laziness as well as the ability to arrive at a decision and follow through with perseverance and persistence until success is accomplished. Additionally, it can be defined as an inner power or drive that helps you to overcome the mental resistance to act.

What's the Difference Between Willpower and Self-Discipline?

Believe it or not, these two are quite different. While willpower is necessary to catapult you into action, you need self-discipline if you truly want to realize your true potential. Self-discipline is the companion of willpower and allows you to be consistent and persevere in whatever you do. It gives you the ability to withstand difficulties whether they are emotional or mental. Additionally, self-discipline gives you the ability to reject instant gratification for the greater good (for something better) even if this requires a lot more effort and time.

Therefore, if you are to develop strong self-discipline and willpower, you ultimately become conscious of your subconscious impulses and acquire the ability to reject them if they cause you to slow down and lose momentum. Self-discipline coupled with strong willpower can allow you to choose your behavior and reactions instead of being enslaved by them. You will start to feel more powerful and in charge of yourself and your surroundings when you muster self-discipline.

Before we start discussing various ways and methods you can use to develop this ability, it is important to first touch on the importance or significance of self-discipline to succeed and discuss reasons why most of us lack this. Delving into these two aspects will help you understand the importance of developing self-confidence.

Why Do You Need Self-Discipline in Life?

When you lack self-discipline, you lack self-control. You do not stay dedicated to your missions and easily lose sight of what is important and beneficial to you. Self-discipline seeks to reverse that; it helps you to stick to whatever it is you have planned to do no matter the level of discomfort or difficulties that you face along the way.

- Self-discipline allows you to exercise control over yourself and avoid thinking or feeling negative. When you are self-disciplined, you think before acting, brainstorm easily, think lucidly, focus on important tasks, easily complete all the chores you have started, and successfully carry out your plans and decisions despite obstacles, hardships, and inconveniences that come your way.

- You start to make the right choices by evaluating situations and by weighing their pros and cons; the opportunity cost factors in because you are momentum driven and strive to complete tasks in as little time as possible. When you are self-disciplined, you seldom make erratic, impulsive decisions.

- You will become happier and more peaceful. A study showed that those who had high self-control are happier as compared to those who lack this ability. They deal with their conflicts a lot better, wasting less time on unhealthy behavior and making positive decisions easily.

- Self-discipline allows you to continue working on a project even when your enthusiasm has faded away. Having the responsibility that you owe yourself and the realization that you alone oversee your destiny allows you to keep going.

- It becomes easier to build character, inner strength, and stability; now it seems more natural to control your impatience, anger, instinctive reactions, and appetite. As a result, it becomes second nature to build and maintain relationships, command respect from others, as well as control your thoughts and reactions, and ultimately achieve everything you've set yourself to do.

Why Is Your Self-Discipline Lacking?

- Have you ever wondered why?

- You decide to watch TV and forego going for a walk even though you know walking is good for you and releases those wonderful endorphins that make you feel great.

- You keep procrastinating on doing something important, like starting a business or asking for a pay raise to justify your true worth, even though you know that this is what you want.

- It seems so daunting to overcome laziness, stop excessive eating, stop smoking, or stop your lack of assertiveness.

Well, the answer is simple: you currently lack the ability to prioritize what is important in life. You do not value the precious commodity of time enough or are just not motivated to improve your situation. These are all the shortfalls of not possessing self-discipline.

Do you often say to yourself, "I wish I could have the willpower and self-discipline to get things done"? If you are aware of what is needed to accomplish your goals, why do you procrastinate?

Let us discuss a few reasons why this appears to be a problem in so many people.

Self-Discipline Is Not an Inbuilt Ability

It is not something you are born with; it is something you work on and develop. You need to work hard to build self-discipline and perfect this strength daily. Never underestimate the power of routine.

Negative Mental and Emotional Programming

Not all of us have positive and healthy programming (mental programming). In our childhood and throughout our lives, many of us go through various terrible incidents that induce negative thinking in us. These incidents shape negative behaviors and keep us from gaining self-discipline.

Negative Environments

A positive environment is mandatory in the development of self-discipline and willpower. If the people that surround you are not supportive and constantly demoralize you, you will never be able to discern right from wrong and discipline yourself. If you don't live in a positive environment, you need to work on creating one for yourself to gain self-discipline.

Fear of Failure

The fear of failing at something often keeps us from taking the initiative. When you cannot initiate tasks and activities, you cannot move toward your goals. This lowers your inner strength, an integral and essential part of developing willpower.

Laziness

If you are incredibly lazy and never feel like doing anything, you will always procrastinate. It will seem much more alluring to take the easy way out and procrastinate even if a task is critical to the attainment of your goals. This is what separates successful people from the masses. To develop self-discipline, you must let go of laziness and procrastination—it is that simple.

Low Self-Esteem and Self-Confidence

When you are not sure of yourself and what you are capable of, you cannot truly value yourself. When you are not aware of your strengths and lack confidence, developing the discipline to get things done can be a great challenge.

Easily Falling Prey to Temptation

If you easily fall prey to different things that lure you away from your goal, then your self-discipline is lacking. It is essential to overcome your weaknesses and temptations to gain restraint and self-will.

A Lack of Purpose

To be self-disciplined, you must have a purpose in life. You must have a goal you look forward to and stay dedicated to. This means that you should not easily be content with your current situation but strive to improve continuously.

By now, you must have probably noticed one or several reasons why you lack self-discipline. So, what can you do in order to transform your life? That's what we will be learning in the subsequent chapters.

Know the Reasons You Want to Gain Self-Discipline

Picking up this book to read is a common starting ground for many people, but the reasons why you want to gain self-discipline will vary as we all have different goals. The most important thing you must establish first is the light at the end of the tunnel. Why do you want to build momentum to transform your life? This should be the main motivation whenever you feel like you are reverting to your old ways.

Visualize Your Objectives (Specify Your What)

You cannot achieve much in life if you don't know what it is you really want. Be specific: if the goal is to lose weight, define how many kilos you would like to lose and within what time period. Next, how will you measure your progress? For this to work, you will need to use the power of visualization to give you a good picture of the version of yourself that you want to become.

To visualize what you truly want, set a specific time when you can sit peacefully with no nearby distractions. Relax and then begin envisioning your goals. Utilize every sense to make the vision you see yourself as real as possible.

Once you have successfully visualized accomplishing your goals, practice simulation, a helpful technique that can help you achieve your set objectives. To exercise it, imagine engaging in all the steps necessary to achieve your goal instead of solely envisioning the result. For example, in the weight-loss scenario, envision eating healthy, exercising regularly, and tracking your performance.

Visualization and simulation can help you make your dream come to life. When you know your ultimate or even short-term desires and imagine yourself achieving them, you become enthused to go after them.

As you know, you need self-discipline to achieve your goals. Visualizing and simulation alone may not help you go far in your quest toward achieving what it is you want. To create the needed spark of self-discipline, you will need to look deep within and ask yourself some honest questions. *Why* do you want whatever it is you've envisioned or simulated? *Why* do you need the self-discipline to make that goal a reality?

Ponder on Why You Want to Develop Self-Discipline and Why You Want What You Want

Do you have a goal that you want to achieve but have noticed that you lack the discipline to get going and fulfill your desires?

For instance, have you noticed that you have stagnated greatly career-wise because you just don't seem to have the motivation and self-discipline to search for new opportunities consistently? Have you wanted to get into a habit of waking up early but find it hard to do because you are "nocturnal"? Do you find it hard to follow any weight-loss program simply because of your soft spot for desserts?

All these are signs of lacking self-discipline. For you to overcome that, your greatest booster is to have a strong enough reason as to why you truly need to transform yourself. Start with sitting alone in a quiet, peaceful place and think about why you truly want to be self-disciplined. From the above and similar questions, you can come up with reasons that are convincing enough to get you going. The best way to get started is to come up with a list of positive reasons that come with being self-disciplined. Think about what you are going to gain when you build your self-discipline (to make this possible, you should define your goals, reasons, or ambitions).

On the other hand, you need to think about the negative effects of doing nothing. What will you lose when you do nothing about your current situation? These two lists will give you a good feeling of what exactly drives you to act.

When you clearly understand why you really want to build your self-discipline, it becomes a lot easier to customize your actions to suit your needs. When you have a clear understanding of why you really need self-discipline, you need to learn how to overcome your excuses.

Do Not Wait for The Right Feeling or Time

It isn't uncommon to come across advice that tells you to do something when it feels right and stop when you don't feel good about it (we are told to follow our gut). Well, unfortunately, this bases our actions on emotions rather than reason, which can be quite unstable and unpredictable. We all have a roller coaster of emotions. However, developing self-discipline is about learning how to get past the barriers that we put for ourselves by waiting for a perfect time to do something.

As you've noted in the first chapter, self-discipline is what keeps you focused on a goal even when you no longer feel enthusiastic about it. This reiterates the fact that emotions shouldn't be a determining factor on whether you will get started on something or not. As such, waiting for the right emotion or time is a wrong approach to developing all the self-discipline that you need in life.

Choosing to work or not to work on a task based on the comfort it offers is the wrong approach to doing anything. It is a tactic that can prevent you from gaining self-discipline.

If you tend to have the thought of waiting for a good time and the right emotion to do something, counter that by revisiting your *why*. Of course, when you were developing your *why* list, you never factored your emotions in that, so why should they be a determining factor when it comes to getting things done? However, how can you overcome the habit of waiting for the right feeling and time?

Use Your Decision-Making Skills
Charles Duhigg, the creator of *The Power of Habit*, clearly explains why it is difficult for us to discipline ourselves. He states that basal ganglia are a portion of your brain responsible for your habitual

behaviors. This part of your brain is related to memories, patterns, and emotions—all the elements necessary for making your habits. The decisions you take are created in your prefrontal cortex. As soon as a certain behavior turns into a habit, we stop making use of our decision-making ability and start functioning on autopilot instead, which is your basal ganglia.

This means that if you are to break a bad habit and build a new or healthy habit, you need to start making decisions very actively. When you do that, it will feel unnatural since your bad behavior has become deep-seated in your personality and you have become accustomed to practicing it. Your brain won't easily accept this change and will resist it from developing. However, you need to keep going if you really want to replace your bad habits with good habits. If you stick to it and accept it as a part of yourself, your mind will soon embrace it without resistance.

For instance, if you must exercise to become fit but laziness has become engrained in your personality, then you won't feel good and right when you decide to work out. But if you don't allow your emotions to be a determining factor as to whether to exercise or not, it will be easy for you to build a habit of exercising regularly and ultimately achieve your goal. One way of keeping yourself going is to chant a mantra to motivate yourself.

Dump Your Habit of Making Excuses

Mental Toughness and True Grit

Next, you need to discard your unhealthy behavior of making excuses for delaying a task. This has everything to do with procrastination. You cannot go far in your quest toward building your self-discipline if you constantly procrastinate. Probably, the reason why you've been struggling over the years to achieve your goals is that you make excuses for not starting (which amounts to procrastination). Here are examples of excuses we use:

- "I won't be able to go for a jog because my jogging partner will not be coming."

- "I won't go to the gym for thirty minutes today because I want to go for one-hour next time."

Well, all these are excuses. However, if you want to transform yourself to a version that gives no excuses, you will need to be very honest with yourself to determine the real reason why you don't want to do something that needs to be done to achieve your goal.

For example, if you come up with the excuse "I won't go out for a jog now because it's too cold outside," then you need to be honest with yourself and state the real reason of not jogging. Instead, tell yourself, "I am not going jogging because I am extremely lazy and lack the will to do something healthy." Ouch! Did that sting? Of course, it did. That's what honesty does. It pinches you and makes you realize your wrongs.

No one wants to admit that they are lazy. This is precisely why this realization will push you out of your self-defined comfort zone of laziness to prove to yourself that you are not guilty of this. With time, it will be easy to transform your life when you stop giving excuses for your inability to act.

The Worst Enemies of Self-Discipline

Goal achievement and success have two great enemies: the path of least resistance and the comfort zone. You are the only one who can convince yourself to put aside instant gratification for the long-term realization of a larger and grander objective. Insofar as the society and everyone else is concerned, your long-term personal goals are of no significance. They would rather prefer that you join them in their fun and games and have a good time yourself.

You can't blame them, for your endeavor to find personal glory is not their concern, just as you couldn't be bothered about which of your acquaintances nurse a personal ambition of becoming an astronaut. As they say, to each their own. You have your journey, and they have theirs. But you can distract each other and get away from your core goals.

The single-minded pursuit of your goal is possible only through employing self-discipline.

Path of Least Resistance

This is the reason that makes people opt for the easy way out all the time. They try to find shortcuts to get everything done. As days go by, they completely buy into the practice of going for the fastest and easiest ways of accomplishing what they want instead of taking the rough road, which is necessary to attain real success.

If you want people to reassure you that you are doing the right thing, you will find plenty of people willing to do that. After all, how would your core goals be of any interest to them? But you will be doing yourself incalculable harm by following this path.

Comfort Zone

This is in addition to the first one. However, it could be considered considerably more detrimental than the last objective since it puts people firmly on the path to failure and incompetence. Unfortunately, however, people usually decide to carry on their business by choosing the easiest and not the best way of doing things. They are not too concerned about the long-term effects of their actions. They only think about what's easy and fun now in time.

Again, this realization must be your own and nobody else's. Moving out of your comfort zone is never easy, but as they say, fortune favors the brave. Ships may look fantastic in the harbor, but their real place is on the high seas. Wallowing in your comfort zone is the easiest thing you can do, but the payoff can be terrible.

Chapter 3:
Starting Out Tips for Self-Discipline

Stay Away from Temptations

A lot of the time, when you're trying to motivate yourself not to do something, you just must keep that temptation away from you.

Not that it's necessarily as simple as that, but straight up avoiding temptation can be useful in getting yourself on track. Even if the thing you're trying to avoid is all you think about during your time away from it, you're still making progress if you can manage to keep your distances.

You may be sitting somewhere, gnashing your teeth, clenching your fists until they're white and praying a Twinkie truck crashes outside your house. But if you don't give in to that sugar craving, it's a total win, and you're one step closer to kicking the habit altogether.

So, don't keep your downfall in your darn house! If you tend to binge on certain junk food, don't have it easily accessible, just hanging out in your cupboard. It will start to call your name, and it's a lot harder to hear it from the store shelf than from your kitchen.

Mental Toughness and True Grit

Similarly, if you always convince yourself you'll just go for one drink at happy hour but always, without fail, end up drunk off doing 90s R&B karaoke in Koreatown, maybe you could stand to skip the after-work drink party occasionally.

Basically, avoid the substances and situations that you know aren't doing you any favors. You can't eat a whole box of Twinkies if they're not there, and you can't drink eight pints and serenade the karaoke bar with the sweet sounds of Boys II Men if you're not there.

You don't have to avoid temptation 24/7. If the theory is true and each time, we use our willpower it weakens just a little bit, *you may want to pick your battles*.

We start the day avoiding doughnuts and not giving our superiors any sass back, but all those instances deplete our self-discipline reserves and chip away at the wall that's holding back our temper or willingness to forgo sweet stuff in favor of something healthy. Exercising self-discipline is great, but sometimes, getting to your breaking point isn't worth it. Treating yourself with the occasional indulgence will help keep those floodgates closed.

That's why the concept of a cheat meal in the fitness world was invented. You work out and eat clean six and a half days out of the week, and then you use one meal to eat what you couldn't the rest of the week. Knowing the cheat is coming makes sticking to your plan for the rest of the week much easier. It's not "Never again." It's just "Later."

It's also a good idea to occasionally give in to temptation when you're trying to kick a habit because going cold turkey can totally backfire. If you completely avoid something until you think you're over it, then reintroduce it somehow, you might be looking at a serious relapse. You haven't learned how to avoid that thing in a healthy way; you just ignore it.

So, when you've gone three months without sugar and decide to indulge in some birthday cake, you'll probably realize how amazing sugar is, how much you missed it, and how easily you could be eating it all the time. Then you do—all the time. And you're back to square one.

Little indulgences help you stay on track and make sure the ban is willpower-based and not an unhealthy mental block.

Life is all about the choices that we make, and therefore, we need to stay focused and motivated until we achieve it. Temptation happens every day, and it can divert us from our goals and achievements. Overspending, overeating, and overdrinking can lead to various complications in our life that can keep us involved in different things that cloud our minds and do not allow us to focus on our goals. Hence, it is important that we know how to resist temptations and stay true to our goals and objectives in life.

Distract Yourself

Mental Toughness and True Grit

Temptation can lure us into things that might seem great, and we might just follow it blindly, but we must have self-control and distract our minds and think of something else. There are many things in life that can distract you, but if you have self-control and willpower, you can think of various different things that matter to you in life, and that way, you can be sure that you never have to give into temptation. For instance, if you are focusing on lose weight, don't go to restaurants where you find junk food. Even if you do visit, make sure you think of something else and keep your mind busy with other important things.

Stick to Your Plans

If you have made plans, make sure that you stick to it, no matter what. Don't change your minds and give in to temptation. Initially, temptations can be hard to resist. This is where you need to be stronger because if you give in once, you'll keep giving in always. Always make plans that can help you to be determined about what you want to do in life and stay motivated to execute those plans.

Stay Busy

If you believe you get tempted easily, you may want to keep yourself busy. This way, you never really have time to sit down and think of things that can tempt you. Things can be controlled in a better way by scheduling your routine so that you get a few minutes for yourself, and then you can call it a day. Although staying too busy can suck out the energy out of you, this will at least keep you motivated and focused, and you can quickly keep up with your plans to achieve your goals.

Talk to Yourself

No one can tempt you, except you. Well, there are many distractions and temptations in this world, but no one has the power to distract you if you don't want to. If you feel tempted, you can always talk yourself out of it. When you get tempted, you usually talk to yourself, and you convince and rationalize to yourself that it's okay to do certain things. Similarly, you can also talk yourself out and ensure that you don't do it, no matter where you are. For instance, if you have decided to quit smoking and you see your friends smoking, you can always tell yourself that you don't have to smoke because it will affect your life negatively.

A Summary of Dealing with Temptations

Temptations are your worst enemy when trying to build self-discipline. Making a commitment is easy. Anyone can devise a plan to achieve something, and everything will seem easy until temptation confronts you.

True self-discipline is best manifested through your triumph against temptations. Resisting temptation is not easy, but it is not an impossible feat. Here are some useful strategies:

- Concentrate on the long-term. Giving in to temptation will satisfy your momentary craving for something, but it will not accomplish your goal. A good way to deal with the pangs of temptation is to remind yourself of the why. Why are you seeking this change or improvement? Why are you trying to build self-discipline? When you focus on the long-term gain, the momentary gain will be immaterial, and you will be stronger against temptations.

- Always be present in the moment. Sometimes you give in to temptation out of impulse. It happens so fast that you don't even have time to think about it. Well, that's where things went wrong—you didn't think. You were completely absent from the moment and didn't have time to pause and think about it. By becoming more self-aware, you open your eyes to everything that is happening. So, when temptations come to distract you, you should be present in the moment so that you can resist it with all you might.

- Be with the social circles you choose to be part of. People exist in different social circles. Some people exist in more than one circle. Study the circles you have and assess whether your circles encourage you to have self-discipline. For instance, if you want to quit drug addiction, then maintaining friendships with drug addicts will not help your rehabilitation. How can you resist drugs if you are constantly in the presence of those substances? Do you think that's healthy?

- Utilize the reward and punishment system. Forming new habits is about learning something. It involves creating a pattern and breaking old habits. Part of this process involves the creation of a working reward and punishment system that you can associate with a specific routine. When temptation hits, you can activate this system and immediately snap out of it.

Watch Your Feelings

As far as negative thoughts go, guilt is often in the middle of all discussions in our minds—guilt about what you should have become, what you should have said, or what you should have done. Unfortunately, these thoughts usually lead to a deep fear, and the guilt may finally become your identity: "I'm a coward," "I can't do that," and "That's not me." Guilt is like cancer for your mind, spreading little by little insidiously to the point where you don't know who you are anymore.

Understanding that everything linked to your guilt is in your past and that you are in total control of your life now is important. You can decide to be who you want to be today. You can decide to take a step forward, even a small one, to change it all. With that choice, guilt can disappear and be replaced by excitement and joy. So how can you let go of these piles of what-ifs and other emotional baggage that prevent you from going forward in your life?

You can't pour from an empty cup. Take care of yourself first.

Mental Toughness and True Grit

I see a lot of people trying desperately to satisfy everybody around them—their boss, their family, their clients. Let me try to help you with this one first. You absolutely don't have to please everyone. I know you might think you have to carry the weight of the world on your shoulders, but you don't. I'm not saying that you need to disinterest yourself from any responsibilities that you have. However, there are two truths in life, and we, as humans, tend to forget from time to time.

First, some problems are not your problem to solve. Your boss has the responsibility to take care of his or her company, not you. Your parents have their responsibilities, too, and they don't need you to fix all their problems. The point is, you don't have to take on problems that are not yours to deal with. You already have enough on your plate. Some people are specialists for imposing their problems on others. They always have something stressful to think about or some dilemma they want you to solve, sucking your energy out as often as they have the chance to. Of course, you want to help them, but understand that you can't help anyone if your mind is already busy solving your own issues and dealing with loads of stress! There is only so much a person can take.

Second, you are not alone in this, and never be ashamed to ask for help or support. We all need it. It's the fools who think they can do everything by themselves, but the truth is that no one can. So, let go of these feelings of failure. You certainly have family and friends to help you in your life. Be proud of that. Be proud that you can reach out to someone you trust, and they will be happy to help you. If you feel like you can't reach out to anyone, go see someone. Yes, you have the responsibility of your life and your problems, but it's written nowhere that you should solve all your problems alone. There is no point in making it worse than it already is.

The point here is to make you understand that you can't help anyone if you don't help yourself first. Making room emotionally in your mind will demand you make sure your feelings are 100 percent yours and not someone else's. Of course, it's very natural to sense the fear or the stress of someone close to you and whom you care about but concentrate on your problems before you go helping others. This is an absolute priority. It's a very simple theory, but simplicity is often the key to the truth.

How do you get rid of these limiting beliefs and build a positive mindset?

It's a common line of questioning among people. How do I get rid of limiting beliefs? How do I switch my thinking so that I only have positive thoughts? How can I stop dwelling on my problems? It's true that limiting beliefs often prevent us from getting what we reach for. They can be the cause of regular failures and disappointments, as we always envision the worst scenarios. Therefore, we end up being fearful, and we have a lack of confidence in certain areas of our life.

Mental Toughness and True Grit

However, I have noticed that only one or two main issues can cause limiting beliefs that create many negative thoughts and consequence. These issues can come from childhood trauma or a mindset that has been taught to you since childhood. And whatever your core fears are, they come as a filter on how you usually see life.

The initial step to doing away with these beliefs is awareness. Being more present in your life and aware of your thoughts and feelings will help you dig down into your mental issues. Ask yourself some simple questions: "Why am I reacting this way?" and "How do I really feel about this?" Reconnecting with yourself will liberate you as you may discover truths and feelings that were buried in your memory. Let me illustrate this with my own story. When I was a kid, I always took care of my sister. My mom was not a bad mom per se, but she liked her freedom. Since I was a responsible child, she felt she could leave me to take care of everything to do with my sister: watching her, playing with her, entertaining her, and even punishing her when she made mistakes. In my mind, I knew all this had happened. I was aware of this past, but I never really understood how it had affected every aspect of my life.

For a long time in my adulthood, I felt like I needed to be in charge, like everyone was counting on me. I never talked about my problems, but I always took care of other people, taking useless charge of everything. The day I discovered all that, I was having some argument with my boyfriend, and I took a moment to ask myself: "Why are you overreacting about this?" (It certainly was a stupid fight. I don't even recall the subject of it.) I was able to really feel that deep guilt I had inside me. It was guilt that stemmed from taking charge of things that didn't belong to me. It was guilt for not being able or strong enough to take on these accountabilities that weren't even my own. Finally, there was anger—real, pure, and honest anger. I realized I wasn't angry at my boyfriend (although he probably may have deserved it!) but at my mom. *She* was the immature one. She was the one running away from her responsibilities, not me. I guess this realization helped me make sense of a lot of failures and stress in my life. In the end, it really liberated me.

I hope you can find what's slowing you down too. If you feel you are always trapped in the same scenario, the same fight, or the same problem, I guess you'll have to search into this first. It doesn't have to be something big, because sometimes our limiting beliefs are built on one story or what someone once said. In the meantime, following the advice of this book will help you get more clarity as you will feel less stressed and more open to your own intuition. So be patient. Everything will come to mind when the time is right—maybe when you are able to listen.

Simplicity should be the keyword of your soul.

We all have problems, and we are all complex beings. We are all busy and stressed out, and we all want to be strong enough to face any situation we meet. So, it's easy to believe that everything is harder than it needs to be. The truth is, you can relax a little bit and just go with the flow sometimes. A lot of problems solve themselves with time. They don't need your full energy.

In the same way you decluttered your life and your space, you also need to declutter what you want to think about. Are these thoughts really yours? Does solving these problems really help you to reach your goals, or are you just trying to please everybody?

When I first realized I put too much pressure on myself at work, it gave me clarity about my problems. They weren't mine. I guess they weren't anyone's. It was just pressure I was putting on myself, hoping to prove something, maybe to my boss or to myself. In the end, there was really no reason for me to do such a thing. I was trying too hard to make a point that I didn't even care about because it just wasn't my purpose.

I invite you to reformulate your problems. What are they all about? What will you gain from all this? What are you trying to prove and to whom? I'm confident these answers will help you find a deeper sense of lucidity and discover simplicity in your mind. Almost every time, stress is caused by a willingness to escape a situation. What are you trying to escape? Believe it or not, life is simple. You care about it, or you don't. If you do care but don't know why, there might lie your fundamental problem. This is what is blocking your mind, and this is what you should be focusing on solving.

Bottom line: You can't help anyone if you don't help yourself first. Seek simplicity in your mind, for it is the only way to reach focus and peace of mind.

Do Not Do What Is Uncomfortable

Self-discipline allows you to pursue your goals without falling prey to various distractions and temptations that will stop you from achieving your goals. You can do this by setting boundaries and learning to say no when the occasion calls for it. Saying yes might be the polite thing to do, but if it is detrimental to your success, then saying no is the best course of action for you.

We'd love to say yes, all the time to people who need us, people who want us to do something for them. Sometimes we might feel like we're being taken advantage of, but we usually shrug these feelings off because we want to please people and hate disappointing them. This is especially true for people who mean a lot to us—like family and friends—and people we look up to, such as mentors and respected members of the community.

Setting Boundaries for Yourself

Boundaries *protect* you from those who'd take advantage of you and your time. It lets you define your space. It lets other people know what's most important to you and how you want to be treated.

Mental Toughness and True Grit

When setting boundaries, you must know what your values and limits are, what you like and don't like, and what you're willing to compromise on. You must stick to your boundaries but, at the same time, be *willing to compromise*, especially if doing so will help you reach your goals faster.

Having boundaries in place keep you honest and real with yourself. You know the situation when to say yes and when you need to say no. If you don't have any boundaries, you'll end up saying yes, all the time. Now there's nothing wrong with saying yes and helping other people, but if you sacrifice too much of yourself and your time, you're left with *nothing* for yourself.

Some people love taking advantage of others they perceive as weak because it makes them feel better about themselves. If you keep on saying yes even when you want to say no, these people are going to continue asking until you finally set boundaries and learn to say no.

Saying No Can Be Diversion to Your Success

Every time you say yes to something that's a *deterrent* or *distraction* from your goal, then you're only making your journey to success *much longer*. It's, therefore, important to note that if you want to reach your goals or your dreams in the shortest amount of time possible, then you must learn to say no.

If you aren't too private a person and you don't mind sharing your long-term goals with others, you can try mentioning your goals to them *as a disclaimer* right before you say no to whatever they are tempting you with.

For instance, if someone is inviting you to go out for a night of partying and drinking and you know that wasting your time on frivolous activities like that won't exactly help you achieve anything, then just tell your friend something like, "Sorry, no, I'm busy tonight."

If you think telling your friend the true reason for your rejection will insult or hurt him, then just say something else and reject them gently (some people can be sensitive to rejection).

Rejecting people is not easy. Sometimes you may even end up debating with someone because they won't accept your rejection and they won't listen to your reasons for saying no. Most of us probably have a few domineering friends like that who thinks they're always right and refuse to listen to opposing arguments.

Getting them to accept your rejection might be hard, but if it brings you a *step closer to your long-term goals*, then, please say no. Strengthening your resolve to say no and standing your ground helps improve your self-discipline and self-control. So, it's definitely a win-win situation for you.

Saying no is hard if you're not used to saying it, but once you start setting boundaries and letting other people know what those boundaries are, then over time, it gets easier and easier to say no. If they trespass your boundaries, then you are well within your rights to tell them off. They might not like it, but they will understand. If they don't, just ask them how they'd like it if *you* stepped on *their* boundaries!

Put Yourself Above Others

It's normal to feel guilty when you disappoint other people, but you must be strong and firm when rejecting someone. If they sense a weakening of resolve, they'll ask you again and again until you give in. If you allow yourself to give in their pestering, then you'll disappoint *yourself*. You're essentially *transferring* the disappointment from them to you, and you don't want to do that because it's not healthy.

It's unhealthy to say yes when you're dying to say no inside. It's never a good idea to agree to something that goes against your beliefs and principles. When you're not committed to doing something wholeheartedly, your performance is going to suffer. You're not going to deliver what's expected. You may disappoint yourself and the person who made you say yes against your will.

If you have boundaries in place, then you'll be putting your needs and yourself ahead of everyone else. Putting yourself above others is an important aspect of self-discipline. If you value yourself and your time, then you must learn how to say no. You must accept that you can't please everybody, and you must believe that you're not a bad person just because you rejected someone.

In the process of building self-discipline and reaching for your goals, you will need to say no far often than you may like. There's no way around this fact, so the earlier you come to terms to rejecting people, the faster you will grow, and the more disciplined you will be.

Just remember that rejection doesn't have to be harsh and rude. In fact, rejection delivered in a kind and gentle manner may result in much better relationships with the people you've rejected.

We need to understand that saying no is not a selfish act. In fact, it can be the very best thing for you, your family, and your other commitments at this time. You can devote more quality time to the things that you've already said yes to, plus your personal needs.

Therefore, people need to prioritize the things that are important to them. They gain time to commit to the things that they want and need to do. One needs to examine his or her current obligations and priorities before making a new commitment.

The fact of meaning and being able to say no, which is not something damaging, is a respectful attitude toward another person who needs some honesty about what is expected from him. Some instances like drug abuse can be caused by peer pressure. In a world in which, for instance, the pressure made by a homogeneous group is one of the factors associated with drug abuse. Just like in other situations of abusive behavior, a person is ethically forced to say no as a necessary limit.

Mental Toughness and True Grit

This will be possible if we get involved in the teaching process from childhood and if we achieve coherence and consistency in our words and behavior. However, group pressure is not always negative.

We are not always persuaded to do something wrong. Sometimes other people can have a point, so the right way to answer back to persuasions is not denial to do what we are asked. For example, adolescents must learn when it is convenient to resist the pressure of their pairs and when it is not. First, they should listen to what they are told, compare it with what we want, and then take the decision, choosing the most convenient one.

In this way, we will avoid impulsive or almost unconscious answers. There is a lot of evidence that the world of "Yes, yes, yes" brings us problems with our work, family, and children: "Do this, do that." "Get more of this, get more of that." "Do not stop." "Keep on moving." "Take this challenge, finish the project, and run to the next meeting." "Find a new client."

To learn to say no, first you must understand what's resisting you to say it. It could be because you were brought up under the notion that saying no, especially to people who are more senior, is rude, as I mentioned above. Sometimes you don't want to alienate yourself from the group, so you conform to others' requests. Or maybe you are afraid the other person might get angry if you reject him or her, leading to an ugly confrontation. Even if there isn't a confrontation, there might be dissent created that might lead to negative consequences in the future. Or perhaps you are worried that saying no means closing doors.

It is necessary to understand that assertiveness does not imply that we must refuse all requests. However, there are times when we have the right to consider our needs before the needs of others and the right to refuse requests made of us.

We could say that we all suffer from a chronic case of If you feel busier than ever, with lots of commitments, you are not alone. We can think that there are two types of yes that contribute to this sense of feeling integrally exhausted.

The first yes emanates from fear. If we say, "There is not enough. I must keep going. I can get over it," the yes is based on the addiction for success, a cultural pattern that models someone's character. Successful people tend to overcommit themselves to something or to do something. They feel the need to say yes to everything. They have a voracious appetite to get more.

There is also this catastrophic tendency: "If I do not say yes to this project, I will not probably be invited to a new one. They are going to think that I am not interested in their ideas. They will look for another person, and there will not be room for me in the future."

Mental Toughness and True Grit

It is not the impulsive, automatic *no* that one offers out of resistance, anger, or stubbornness. It is a different kind of *no*. It comes from understanding and accepting who we are and who we are not. It comes from knowing what is true for you and what is false. This no is a sign of respect for yourself, recognition that it is perfectly fine to be who you are; you do not have to disguise, distort, or reject your truth.

Frequently, we say yes and either instantly regret it or realize somewhere along the way we have done it again and end up feeling stressed and out of control or worn out.

It could be argued that we don't know how to say no assertively; we weren't taught to say no in ways that don't hurt the feelings of others. We weren't taught to value saying no.

There are two types of *no*.

The first type is our inner enemy that tells us: "You cannot. You will not do fine." This inner enemy talks to us to make us weak, and we often do not know how to hold it back. That is the reason why I have just sent a friend an e-mail so that he stops thinking that the solution lies in taking medicines to avoid stress.

The second no means "I can do it, but I choose not to do it." This *no* is powerful and difficult because it reaches what it is called the prime of life: knowing what is important, choosing what to do and what not to do. This person has learned to live out of the common limits just for saying no.

- "I won't travel just anywhere I have been asked to."

- "I won't visit this organization."

- "I do not eat what you usually eat."

- "I won't get back home late."

- "I won't turn on the computer so that I can talk to my child."

- "I do not stand up when my friends are talking even when they are saying something that does not make sense."

- "If they have made me think or made me laugh so many times, why should I leave?"

- "I won't speed up while driving just because others hurry me up."

- "I turn off my mobile phone two hours a day because nobody will die if I cannot be contacted and because if something is supposed to occur, it will happen regardless of whether I get the phone call at that moment or not."

We must understand the search process of our own "yes" that lives in the dissatisfaction that we have of the world, a world confronted with a lack of harmony and conflicts. This search cannot appear like

Mental Toughness and True Grit

a reduction, so we must learn that selfishness (which is good if it favors us) keeps us away from others.

Furthermore, we need to understand that we can support our behavior when it fulfills two conditions: Everybody in any place or circumstances can realize it. This learning process should start at an early age.

Childhood is an excellent moment in human development not only for the child but also for the adult. Children's attitudes confront adults with several dilemmas. It is part of children's behavior to refuse something or rebel against something.

The best way that the child must become more self-confident is to oppose. It is a way child must establish a difference between themselves and the outside. It is a defense against the feeling of invasion they perceive from the constant requests they have from their environment.

Lately, this process recovers its strength in adolescence and can turn into concrete and specific behavior. The problem for the adults lies when this tendency becomes an excess; and because of shyness, comfort, or pragmatism, it can become a habit.

Many adults suffer when they must refuse to do something, either because they are afraid of letting down other people's expectations or because they are afraid of not knowing how to support their denial or just because of laziness or comfort.

It is the fear of not being valued or loved. Our need to be valued, looked after, and considered can lead us from the mirage that fosters low self-esteem to show a constant predisposition toward everything. Therefore, this situation leads us to dependency not only on other people but also in the image from which we move, leaving aside our right to say no.

We need an equilibrium that let us be tolerant and understanding while giving us space to express our nuances or disagreements. If we always give ground, we hurt ourselves. If we are not able to say no, we will think that the same may happen to others.

Our choices, either for yes or no, require to be on alert, attentive. They require to listen, observe, give time, and understand if it is yes or no, avoiding the affirmative just to get by. It is not easy to say no.

In this process, we will discover sincerity and manipulation. They are inner processes that show our inner world. Some people say that they are related to our behavior boundaries, if it is so, they are in the domain of ethics. We are quite a lot the ones who have had to unlearn the fortuitous, comfortable, and indifferent yes; and in fact, we have done so in our deepest silence.

Mental Toughness and True Grit

Immanuel Kant celebrates the systematic development of willingness through discipline. He ignores the voices of instinct, of the curious conscience in fear of the weakness of character that leads us to a life anchored on the whim.

When we face a situation that demands a yes or a no, our restlessness may take us at the ends of the question, take us to shake our most inner fibers, and examine our certainties.

It is very important to say no politely when the circumstances are suitable, but with determination and arguments—that is with an elaborated linguistic code. That is the reason why it is important to get involved in the situation of the person who is going to get a no for an answer.

We can say no nicely. For example, "I like you, and I really wish I could be there for you, but I just can't right now." If you don't know the person well, a simple "No, thank you" suffices. Individuals are different, and what works for one person may not work for you. Therefore, one can use different ways to say no. There is an easy way, but some people forget to try it: Say, "No, thanks," then give a reason, fact, or excuse. You can also use humor.

There exist several explanations about why it is hard for us to say no. Of course, this depends on the situation and the person as well. There are situations in which it is almost impossible to say no. For example, when your boss "asks" you to stay in a very important meeting after you have finished your work. There are other situations in which it is easier to say no. One instance is when somebody wants money back for cleaning the window screen of your car.

Reward Yourself

Rewarding yourself from time to time for the efforts taken is a good habit to adopt and a key part of the process that shouldn't be overlooked. Why, you may wonder?

Because rewarding yourself motivates you and inspires you to continue acting. By rewarding yourself, your mind will unconsciously start associating good feelings with finishing tasks. In other words, your mind will start relating positive rewards to each effort that you take. Do not allow your ego to run your life. You will find plenty of stories about rich people with deep regrets of not balancing their work with breaks. Work smarter, not harder. I sit back and smile when people declare they are the hardest workers (working sixteen to twenty hours a day for active income), never sleep, and how much they love the grind. "Have fun," I tell them. I'll be the most efficient worker. I set up my businesses to grow while I sleep, gaining passive income, and I will enjoy the grind from a place of want, not need. That's a long-term winning mindset.

Successful people reward themselves from time to time so that the effort feels worthwhile. You see, it does you no good if you fail to reward yourself because as time goes by you may start getting a feeling of burnout and lack of desire to act. This is especially true if you had to push yourself harder to act. Therefore, coming up with a reward system is mandatory if you desire to be successful.

How then do you begin rewarding yourself? Rewarding yourself is straightforward. But if you are a workaholic or simply lack ideas, this chapter will discuss a few different methods you can use to reward yourself.

Method 1: Go Out on A Small Trip

The first method that you should consider is that of taking yourself out. It doesn't matter how much you love the work you do. If you do it incessantly without taking even a small break, you will eventually burn out.

Going out on a small vacation is a good way to break off and renew your enthusiasm and energy and recharge your batteries. People who take frequent breaks become happier, calmer, and less stressed than those who do not. In addition, it helps you put things in focus.

There are many places one can visit. You could try museums, malls, aquariums, open-air markets, the beach, or any other place that is out of your normal routine. A good time to take small vacations like these is during weekdays when people are typically at work. During these times, these places are less crowded.

Always keep it short. Somewhere between two to four days is ideal. A short vacation will get rid of the fear that gropes you when you imagine getting back to a mountain of work.

Method 2: Buying Your Favorite Food

Another great way to reward yourself is by treating yourself to your favorite food. When it comes to food, we all have our personal preferences of what we like best. What better way to reward all that discipline to get that work done than to simply go out and buy that food that you've craved for recently.

Thus, go out and grab that ice cream. Drink a glass of wine. Eat that pizza or that cake. You could even cook your favorite meal if you wanted to. It doesn't matter what you prefer. You'll have to decide for yourself on this one, if it's something that you don't often consume so that it ends up feeling special to you once you take it.

Method 3: Reward Yourself with Self-Care

Taking care of yourself is another way to reward your hard work and good behavior. We all love ourselves and would like to look and feel good. Making this part of your reward system can be an extremely powerful way of getting things done and becoming more self-disciplined.

There are countless ways of rewarding yourself with self-care. I will highlight a few ways so that you can get the idea and come up with unique ideas of your own. Some good ways of caring for yourself include the following:

- Going out and getting a manicure/pedicure

- Getting a new tattoo or piercing

- Eating out with a friend and ordering whatever you desire on the menu

- Doing any activity that makes you feel free or like a child (e.g., amusement parks, concerts)

- Getting a massage at your favorite parlor

- Watching a great movie

Method 4: Take Yourself Out for Some Shopping

Another way that might work and make you feel good about yourself and strive to work better is to go out for some shopping, although I wouldn't recommend reckless spending that would drive you to debt or make your broke. Some of us just want our money to feel better than just numbers in the bank. You may want to compensate for that feeling by buying something.

For this reason, I will recommend one way of getting around the problem of overspending.

I recommend setting up a rewards account. This is like a savings account, only meant for buying rewards for yourself. Periodically, put some money into this account and reserve it for when you accomplish tasks successfully. Then, once you hit a significant milestone, you can dig into your rewards account and take yourself out for some shopping.

This will help you avoid overspending and still allow you to buy things for yourself as a way of making yourself feel good.

Method 5: Treat Yourself to Something Fun but Free

While buying yourself things like food, clothes, items, and vacations are great ways for rewarding yourself, you don't have to make it all about money. All things considered; I would always advise that you seek ways of rewarding yourself that will involve little to no money. That way, you won't risk your financial freedom or stability. Always finding an excuse to spend money is not a great way to financial prosperity. Here are several ways you can reward yourself and not spend money:

- Try going to a nice park/landmark in your town and enjoy nature

- Attend a free social event

- Play a video game at home

- Take a small nap

- Go out and take photos or videos

With some bits of creativity, you could come up with great ways to have fun but still avoid spending money.

All in all, this chapter has to some degree provided you with great ideas of rewarding yourself. Rewarding yourself is a great and fun part of cultivating self-discipline. Being mentally tough is good, and this book has covered a huge part of doing that. However, what is even more important so that the good habits stick is to reward yourself consistently. It provides the much-needed incentive to keep pursuing your goals on your way to success.

Forgive Yourself and Move Forward

In order to prosper in the "outer world," you must first discipline yourself to assess your best options. Focus on the things you so wish to chase after. Pursue action steps toward your goals. Work hard to achieve those goals and finally emerge as a more capable and better person.

Divergently, in order to succeed in the "inner world," you must first discipline yourself to let go of all that you suspect will disrupt your state of inner peace and happiness. In other words, you must choose to let go of all the things you obsessively attach with and want to conquer.

You see, although you've achieved a level of monetary success, significance and status are all things that can make you feel content and satisfied in the outer world. If you do not know how and when to manage and even detach yourself from these worldly pleasures, you're likely to feel confused and burdened by the sheer responsibility of this newfound success.

Ironically, while most people spend the best of their adult and middle age battling the harshest of competition in search of significance and certainty, they spend their remaining years seeking ways to let go of the very qualities they fought for before. The key leading to a fulfilling and happy life is to find a balance between material and spiritual mastery.

Almost all spiritual teachings attribute attachment as the main cause of human suffering and unhappiness. When people become increasingly attached to their ideas, opinions, and material possessions, they find it difficult to face up to failures or let go of their possessions when the time has come. They identify only with their material success and, therefore, end up feeling guilty, unworthy, and rejected without it. What's worse is that they harness a sense of blame and refuse to forgive themselves for the rest of their lives. In fact, this is one of the primary reasons for depression and human suffering across the world.

The key to finding the balance is to practice detachment. Separate yourself emotionally from any or all the negative outcomes you're likely to face in pursuit of your goals. Only then will you be able to enjoy the levels of success you're about to enjoy without feeling guilty or weighed down by it. You will also be in a position to find inner and outer peace and, with it, find the true purpose of your life.

Forgive Thyself

As per the law of evolution, every person—including you—will have to experience some form of painful memories in their lifetime. While the degrees of pain might differ from person to person, we all will have to undergo some form of criticism, negative treatment, unkindness, rudeness, unfairness, betrayal, or dishonesty as we evolve higher in the spiritual plane.

While these events might be unfortunate, they become the essence of how your character is shaped in the future. In fact, at its heart, these experiences are there to teach you a lesson or two in life, lessons on acceptance and forgiveness.

It's never easy to make a commitment, whether big or small; and when you finally make one, there's always a likelihood that you will slip. Throughout your journey, you will stumble, and you will struggle to remain disciplined, but that doesn't mean that you have failed yet. One slip does not mean the end of the line. One slip is not a dead end that you cannot turn around from.

Self-discipline is best exhibited by your willingness to get back in the game even after you fall. After enduring a horrific failure, you need to be strong enough to forgive yourself so that you can move forward from what has happened.

You see, the height of spirituality lies in the act of forgiveness. Forgive yourself for all that you are guilty of. Forgive yourself for not achieving all that you could have otherwise achieved. Forgive yourself for feeling you were not able to measure up to others' expectations. Forgive yourself for every painful memory that you hold yourself responsible for.

But how can you forgive yourself? You have done so much to get to where you are, and you lose all advantage because of one mistake—that's dreadful. Regardless of what has happened, though, you need to find the heart to forgive yourself because you deserve to be forgiven. No one is meant to be tied to the past forever, and you surely do not deserve to be tied to the mistakes you made before. There is nothing wrong with failure because there's so much to learn from it, and its true meaning is really about perspective. A mistake, however big, can be significantly instrumental to your growth and development.

If you encounter people who say otherwise—those who might say, "I told you so"—do not listen to them. People can force their opinions on you, but they are worth nothing unless you let those opinions matter. Of course, you must consider what other people say, but you shouldn't let them affect you. You need to have the discipline to handle such situations so that they do not overcome you.

Forgive yourself despite what has happened and find the silver lining. Your failure does not have to be the end of the line and could, in fact, be pivotal to your success.

Remember that you are not to be blamed. Instead, I urge you to take only the positives out of every learning curve and utilize it in your journey to the next one.

Give Up Your Suffering

As ironic as it might sound, many people fall in love with the process of suffering. They become addicted to the habit of reliving their past and virtually reenact every painful memory they've encountered repeatedly as if to reverse the outcome or justify the negative emotions they harness inside. Well, they don't. If anything, they only feel worse and add to their list of worries and suffering.

Do not be one among them. Let go of your painful memories and stop justifying the negative emotions that are continuously weighing you down. Remind yourself that "stuff like that" happens in life. Discipline yourself to give up your suffering. Think only about the positive things you've achieved in life and use those expansive memories to enrich your life.

Finally, as I urge you to think about all that I've spoken about in this chapter, I ask you to take a test to see if you have healed at all. Again, if after taking the test, you feel the need to heal and forgive, then I urge you to do exactly so and let go of the demons once and for all. Doing so will leave you feeling liberated and enriched from within.

Take the forgiveness test.

Chapter 4:
Discipline Your Mind like a Navy SEAL

Discipline Is Not A Punishment

Have you ever been disappointed by the fact that you lacked self-discipline? You are not alone. You might know how important it is when it comes to achieving one's goals, so it can be frustrating to realize that it has not developed into a habit. You may even have exhibited self-discipline in the past but keeping that momentum on a roll is a struggle.

Why Is It So Hard?

Self-discipline requires effort and constant hard work. Successful and productive people are not born with it. Rather, they developed self-discipline by determined action and by making the sacrifices no one else can or will. You also need to put in as much effort as they do.

Although there are no shortcuts, it would be easier to develop self-discipline if you know why you want it. Consequently, you should not let challenges stop you from persevering.

Peers

Another reason why you could be struggling with self-discipline is your peers. There may be too much negativity in your peer groups without enough positivity to balance it out. The people you surround yourself with have a far greater influence on you than you may realize, and we will be exploring that later in the book.

Have a quick think about the people that are currently in your life right now. Can they help you stay motivated? How do they view the world? Are they always in search of ways to improve and better themselves? Often, we do not give enough thought to the relationships and the people who make up our circle. With our goal of self-discipline, that circle needs to be reevaluated and perhaps even redefined.

Laziness

Laziness is an enemy of productivity and self-discipline. Moreover, the pull and allure of laziness are so strong that succumbing to it is frighteningly easy. The minute you get sucked into the cycle of laziness, getting out can be very difficult.

It certainly does not help that laziness is often accompanied by procrastination. Combining these two qualities often leads to disaster. They are the deadliest habits any person could have and are usually the very reasons why you are failing. Like an invisible force that is pulling you to the dark side, laziness is an enemy that you will often battle against on your mission to become a more self-disciplined individual.

Letting Go

Difficulty in letting go of the past is another reason why you may be struggling with self-discipline. Past failures and setbacks have a way of haunting you. They have a way of making you doubt yourself. These past events can leave you in doubt and cripple you with the thought of repeating those same failures. These problems are often enough to push many to give up. Developing self-discipline requires letting go of the past. Do not let it be the anchor that weighs you down. Cut yourself loose right now, and do not let it hold you back for a moment longer.

Procrastination

Another enemy of self-discipline is thinking that you have all the time in the world. Of course, that is not the truth. "Time and tide wait for no man," says the adage. Time will not slow down for you. Before you know it, a moment would have come and gone, and a potentially valuable opportunity may have already been missed. Thus, never fall into the trap of thinking that time is in abundance and procrastination is acceptable. We can never know what might happen along the way.

Without self-discipline, it becomes easy to lose the sense of urgency to accomplish a goal or a task that you set for yourself. Temptations are all around you, and the desire to give in can often feel inescapable. You've got electronic devices, streaming services, social media, games, and so much more. There's no shortage of excuses and reasons to procrastinate. It's a constant inner struggle; however, you must let self-discipline win. More on procrastination will be discussed later.

Comfort Zone

Comfort zones are yet another dangerous territory and contribute to the struggle of applying self-discipline. The problem is in the name itself: *comfort*. Why would you ever want to leave a place of comfort and head toward a challenge? With this mindset, you will always struggle to hold onto self-discipline. Complacency can set in, and you will end up always finding excuses to avoid applying yourself. Comfort zones are not inherently bad. However, you should never let yourself become complacent because you then run the risk of losing the desire to do anything at all. Instead, learn to love a challenge.

Never Procrastinate

Everyone has moments when they want to get something done, but instead of working on it, they decide to do it later. Sometimes, the job doesn't interest you that much, and you don't care about it enough to focus on it. Other times, even if you do love the job, you still catch yourself doing other stuff. There are so many ways to delay success in your life, and one of them is procrastination.

For many of us, our first real brush with procrastination comes in school and college when we often put off preparing for tests and examinations until the very last moment. No matter how brilliant you

Mental Toughness and True Grit

might be, it is not possible to perform to full potential until you put in a certain number of hours of detailed study.

It is often the kids who display great discipline in their approach to studies who end up scoring high marks. They may not be the most brilliantly inspired of the lot, but they are certainly bright enough to use the right amount of focus where it is required.

Procrastination is when you postpone or put off important tasks in your daily life. It's a force that stops you from pursuing things that you need to do. It reflects your struggle when it comes to self-control and your inability to anticipate how you will feel the following day. When you don't feel like working on a certain project, it will eventually open doors for negative emotions that will avert the succeeding effort.

In the old days, when religion played a far greater role in people's lives, the preachers lay certain guidelines for living life in a manner that would bring them peace and happiness. That is how you had the concept of the seven deadly sins being presented to people to let them know what kind of behavior would bring them down. Sloth, one of the seven deadly sins, is like procrastination in the sense that you put off doing something, though the reason may not necessarily be laziness. You may, for example, do it out of fear of failure.

But then if you don't have the courage of your conviction to risk inability to achieve your heart's real desire, what sort of a man or woman are you? Procrastinators often undermine themselves. They block their path of success and choose to jeopardize their performance. Why do they do that? Some experts may just have an answer to that.

- About 20 percent of people consider themselves as constant procrastinators. They see procrastination as a lifestyle, although a dysfunctional one. They miss many opportunities to buy concert tickets. They do Christmas shopping at the last minute. They don't settle their bills on time.

- Procrastination doesn't have anything to do with improper planning or time management. Procrastinators can estimate their time. They just appear to be more optimistic compared to other people. In fact, a psychology professor said, "Telling someone who procrastinates to buy a weekly planner is like telling someone with chronic depression to just cheer up."

- People are not born procrastinators. Procrastination is something that they learn indirectly at home. It's one of the ways people respond to authoritative parents. Controlling parents prevent their children from being able to correct themselves and to incorporate within themselves their personal intentions and act. Procrastination can also be an act of rebellion. Under this kind of environment, procrastinators find support from their friends, who are more likely to tolerate their reasons.

- Procrastinators often lie to themselves. They will say that they feel like doing things the next day or that they work best under pressure, and it makes them much more creative. But the truth is, they still don't get the job done. They tend to identify things to be not that important.

- There are different reasons as to why people procrastinate. There are three kinds of procrastinators. First, there are the so-called thrill seekers or arousal types. They wait until the last minute and enjoy the delightful rush. The second category is the avoiders. They try to avoid their fear of disappointment, failure, or even success. They are afraid of what others might think of them. They prefer to let people think that they just don't want to put in effort rather than lack the ability. Third, there are the decisional procrastinators. They have a hard time making decisions. Not coming up with a decision would spare them from being responsible for what might happen.

- Procrastinators always search for distractions, especially things that don't necessarily need much of their commitment. They always check emails or their phone. Being distracted is their way of controlling what they feel, such as feeling like a failure.

- Procrastination can be eliminated but learning how not to do it takes a lot of mental energy. One doesn't necessarily feel the need to transform on the inside. Cognitive behavioral therapy (a type of psychotherapy that changes dysfunctional behaviors, thoughts, and emotions to treat problems and promote happiness) can help achieve it.

Phew! That sure was one detailed analysis of the dynamics of procrastination, but it was important to get to know that so that you realize that chronic procrastinators are not as unusual as you think but are regular people like you and me. Possibly you recognized yourself in some of the situations described above.

Everything starts with a choice. You can either start working on a given task at hand or do something else, such as getting involved with more fun activities or maybe do nothing at all. What drives you to decide to put in an effort into something is based on how much you appreciate completing the job in that moment. As for procrastination, what happens when doing something else has more worth than working on what's important right now? That's crazy right, but then normal is often dull!

If this is the case for you, there's a way to beat procrastination. Try to think of ways to increase the value of your project or lessen several other things that can distract you. You could also combine the two in a more balanced manner. Thinking about how much closer your deadline is could also be another way to expand its worth.

Mental Toughness and True Grit

Feeling the deadline pressure is as good a way as any to lessen the stranglehold of procrastination on you. If the fear of an impending deadline galvanizes you into action to the extent that you work late into the night, you are beginning to see self-discipline making an appearance in your life. This will reinforce itself if this newfound sense of discipline helps you meet the deadline that was almost upon you.

People often tend to procrastinate when they feel like they must put in a whole lot of effort into achieving something. In fact, studies have found that mental exertion is internally harmful in the sense that it introduces an element of ennui that immobilizes you. This reason alone makes people prefer to accomplish easier tasks rather than harder ones. This usually leads to people procrastinating more when they expect work to be challenging to complete—a real vicious circle if there ever existed one.

Procrastination also comes from insufficient identification with the future self. When people have the drive to keep a favorable self-concept, their work tends to have higher value since their goals are personally connected to them. This is the crux of the whole concept of self-discipline. You need to rise above your basic physiological desires and aim higher to be able to begin to put self-discipline into practice.

Ironically, sometimes perfectionists are procrastinators. It is not that they are afraid of hard work; it is because they would rather procrastinate than create something that falls short of perfect. So, they prefer not to take on a task so that they can avoid the chances of failing. Procrastinators usually have their ways of explaining why they choose to put things off. Still, there's a bright side to it. With the right effort, it's indeed possible to defeat procrastination.

But such people can be brought around to instill self-discipline in themselves if they can understand that even perfection can be nearly achieved if one works in a disciplined manner. In fact, the more disciplined you are, the greater your chances of achieving it.

Steps to Stop Procrastination

There's always a deadline to catch. You still end up doing other various things, such as checking emails and surfing the net or social media instead of finishing your work. There's always work that you need to do, but you don't feel like doing anything at all.

You feel like you are running on a treadmill that is never going to stop, so you want to opt out by doing nothing. Sometimes you don't even want to get out of bed, let alone work hard at achieving some obscure long-term goal. Sound a little like you?

The truth, however, is that, for the most part, we are ourselves responsible for the soup we find ourselves in. Procrastination is surely a familiar situation for everyone. You like wasting your free time and setting aside important tasks until it's too late. When it already too late, you start to panic and wish you had done things earlier. You keep on delaying things, slacking, and doing it repeatedly. This terrible habit stops you from achieving bigger goals in life.

Don't allow procrastination to get the best of you. There are different effective ways to stop it. Whenever you're faced with procrastination, you can practice doing these thirteen things to help you get started and kick off your momentum.

Simply Take the First Step

As Martin Luther King Jr. once said, "You don't have to see the whole staircase. Just take the first step." When you immediately look at the end goal, the journey in doing any work can appear to be impossible. This tends to overwhelm you and shuts you down, turning to other things to waste your time. Ensure that you come up with a plan for your future and then slip your attention back now.

Remember, the journey of a thousand miles begins with a single step. You don't take that first step fearing what lies ahead; you'll never achieve anything that way. Just focus on taking the first step. This puts you in a mental state where you get to be more open and positive. Although you're not entirely keen about the following steps you're going to take after the first one, at least you're embracing it. This continuously leads you to take the next step.

Even though you can't get a glimpse of the whole staircase, you'll eventually get there at the end. You'll discover things, which may seem to be far more than your expectations. Unless you move forward, how will you ever realize what you might encounter?

Focus on One Thing at A Time

Just like people always say, success doesn't happen overnight. Everything takes time. Developing self-discipline is the same as building your muscles. It takes a while before you see the results. Every time you train yourself, you take a step forward toward becoming stronger. Although regarding exercising, you could hurt yourself and experience a setback if you push yourself too hard.

Sometimes, things can be a bit overwhelming when you set your eyes on the big goal. This can often lead to procrastination. You need to take it a step at a time. Break down your job into small tasks and focus on each one of them one at a time. Your work will appear simpler, and it will be easier for you to work on it. Having a more realistic goal will take you closer to the big ones. You can enjoy that sense of accomplishment once you're done working on the smaller parts of your job.

Know the Things That Motivates You and What Doesn't

Start by learning more about yourself. Sometimes, fighting off your cravings and urges can be hard. Be aware of the areas where you may tend to struggle more and think of ways to avoid being stuck in those situations. If you simply can't resist having a slice of cake, ice cream scoop, or fries, then keep yourself away from those. You won't be tempted if you don't have them within your reach. If pressuring yourself doesn't work, then put yourself in a place that will help you build self-discipline instead of weakening it. Get rid of the temptations by surrounding yourself with things that will encourage you to achieve your goals.

Know the things that inspire you and light up the fire in you. Your self-control can swiftly go up and down alongside your energy levels. Playing lively music helps to pick up your pace. Teach yourself how to be motivated enough to enjoy doing your chores. Implement these suitable activities into your daily routine. It will be easier for you to develop self-discipline.

Once you have seen that it is possible to exercise self-discipline in the case of things that you are passionate about, you can next begin to apply the same kind of discipline to others area as well. With time, discipline will become your default mode.

Put Yourself in A Different Environment

Different surroundings affect your productivity in a variety of ways. Does your room or work desk make you feel excited to work, or does it make you feel tired and sleepy? If you find your workplace very annoying, maybe it's time to do some changes. Boredom only invites procrastination.

It's important for your environment to make you feel inspired. Some workspace can be motivating at first but will soon lose its effectiveness after some time. This is usually a big problem for people who go to work in the same settings every single day. If you're one of those stuck in this situation, you should think about making some changes to your space.

Moving around now and then can freshen up your surroundings. It can help break the tediousness. It also helps stimulate the mind and increase your enthusiasm. You can also try visiting the library or going to coffee shops or parks when you read or write. A healthy and stimulating environment will create appropriately positive thoughts in your mind, making it far easier for you to practice discipline.

Start by Doing the Hardest Task

Dale Carnegie said, "Perform the hard tasks first. The simple jobs will take care of themselves." Your first hour of the day sets the pace for the entire day to come. A good way to start the morning is to face your most difficult chores for the day first; do the projects that you feel like you would no longer have enough energy to deal with later in the day.

Heavy tasks can include answering big piles of emails, paying the bills, or finishing the last pages of your report. Whatever it is that seems a stack of pain early in the day, go ahead and do it to get it out of your way as soon as possible.

This habit might just keep your day going from dreadful to delightful. That sense of accomplishment will surely help you carry out easier and lighter loads throughout the day. You are more relaxed when you feel like you're improving from time to time.

If you can exercise enough self-discipline to do the heavy lifting first, you will find that performing any routine task will become quite comfortable for you, and you will have cast procrastination aside and become a more engaged and with it.

Drop Perfectionism

Perfection is, indeed, pointless if you want to have a productive day. Perfection is one of the primary reasons why people procrastinate. Eric Thomas sums it up: "There will never be the perfect time to do a great thing." In fact, many successful people know this. They don't allow perfectionism to open doors for procrastination.

You might often hear people saying that there's no such thing as perfect. Although you can always keep on improving, you should not strive for perfection. You just always must put your best effort in anything you do. If you keep waiting for the right time to do things, you might never get anything started. You'll just find yourself in a rush to get things done when you're already faced with a deadline.

It doesn't matter whether you're inexperienced or unprepared. The important thing is to jump right into action. Anything you work on can certainly be developed as time goes by.

Like the tag of a major sports shoes advertising campaign says: "Just do it." How well you perform or how close you come to perfection can be looked at later.

Engage in New Activities or Sports

One of the great ways to build self-discipline is by playing sports. Sports can train you regarding goal settings. It helps you get physically fit, focus on your emotional and mental strengths, as well as get along nicely with other people. Engaging yourself in sports brings you to a place where you can learn real hard work, and always aim to give your best effort. This will train you to incorporate the same ideas and discipline you need in your daily life.

Look at the lives of the greatest sportsmen of our times and, indeed, all times, and you will see how it was mainly unparalleled focus, self-discipline, and hard work that got them to where they eventually arrived.

Many of them came from extremely humble backgrounds with next to no support system, yet they made sacrifices and exercised the self-discipline of the highest possible order to never lose sight of their exalted goals and got there. Take a leaf out of the page of these achievers. It will open your eyes.

Anything that lets you fuel your passion and excel in it must come with self-discipline. Take up something that gets your pulse racing. See how you can leverage that with the help of self-discipline and obtain your goal in life.

If you need other fun events to develop self-discipline, you can also try learning how to play a new instrument, like a guitar or piano. It's a vital thing to master focus, reiteration, and application. Practicing and attaining self-discipline in various areas of your life refreshes your mind and alters it to choose what's right instead of what's easy.

Remove Your Procrastination Stopovers

If you think you're excessively procrastinating, maybe you surround yourself with things that allow you to procrastinate. For instance, if you go on for hours surfing the net, you might need to clean up your bookmarks and put them in folders that will be less accessible. Turn off your notifications if you must. Some people even feel the need to deactivate their social media accounts. The key thing is being aware of your actions to address procrastination.

Removing distractions in your workplace can help keep you from procrastinating, especially when you need to finish important tasks at hand. This way, you give your undivided attention to things that matter. You'll be able to work faster and commit fewer errors.

You cannot let yourself be enervated by distractions, whatever these may be—friends who are easy-going, your virtual world buddies, gossip mongers, eternal pessimists, or whoever will take you away from a disciplined path.

Surround Yourself with People Who Inspire You

Many successful people in their chosen field have always maintained their greatness because they are willing to work so hard at their craft. Their focus and discipline put them at the top of their game. If it used to work for them, it could also work for you.

Surely, spending a few minutes of your time talking to Michael Jordan or Steve Jobs will make you more inspired or motivated to act rather than spending those few minutes doing absolutely nothing. The people you hang out with can significantly influence your behaviors. You don't necessarily have to be with famous people you look up to, like Bill Gates or Steve Jobs for that matter. Only know who among your friends or colleagues are the go-getters and hard workers. Spend time with them. You'll eventually instill their kind of spirit and drive into your life as well. You can also make use of social media to interact or communicate with those who inspire you. It still works the same. Many individuals can be a source of inspiration to you. What you need to do is hang out with them rather than the nay-sayers.

Share Your Goals with Others

Tell your family, friends, and colleagues about your goals. Announce the things you plan to do or want to achieve to the public. Most of the time, peer pressure is seen in a negative way. People associate it with teenagers who are most likely to develop some bad habits in life. However, if you use peer pressure right, it can be a highly effective way to put an end to procrastination.

Mental Toughness and True Grit

Thinking about the way your friends or family will react if you fail at your projects can motivate you to work harder. Use your fear of disappointment to push yourself. Even when you totally don't want to do something, you'll catch yourself acting on it because you don't want to let anybody down and be a complete failure. At least when they see you, they will ask about an update on your plans. It's also a good way to make use of social media when you post about your work. You can keep yourself responsible regarding your daily activities. By sharing your goals with those whose opinion matters to you, you put positive pressure on yourself to perform, which, in turn, necessitates your achieving a sense of self-discipline.

Review Your Goals

Your goals in life are your sources of inspiration and motivation. When you think about them clearly in your head, the fewer chances you have of procrastinating. You strive to work hard because you want to reach those goals. If procrastinating takes so much of your time, it can only mean that what you're doing is not something that you feel like would help you toward achieving what you want.

It might be time to look back and see if you have big and bright enough goals. Maybe all you need is to take a quick break and go on a weekend vacation to reorganize yourself. Revisit your goals. You can write them down and return to them occasionally. It helps to remind yourself what your goals are every single day. You'll be more likely to take the steps toward achieving them.

Viewed with a fresh perspective, your goals appear to be a lot more within your grasp, and you can redirect your energy and focus toward trying to achieve these. This will encourage you to muster your sense of discipline once again and get on with the task of achieving your cherished aims.

Don't Overthink and Just Start Doing It

Planning can be helpful if you want to achieve great things in life. However, too much thinking and planning can only make you do just the opposite.

Some people try so hard to create their perfect plan. They come up with goals where they make sure they won't commit any mistakes or be rejected by others. They make easy and painless plans, but the thing is that it's something no one else can ever do. You can't escape mistakes and failures. Instead, treat it as a stepping-stone for reaching your goals. If you have a good plan and you stick with it, you don't need to worry about anything else.

Overanalyzing and hairsplitting are the best recipes for procrastination, leading to indiscipline. Don't fall into the trap but carry on with your onward path one step at a time until you reach where you want to be. You need to maintain strict discipline and not get off the road that you have decided for yourself.

See the Bigger Picture

Mental Toughness and True Grit

Some people tend to fail at what they do because they forget why they are doing the work in the first place. It's more likely that you will procrastinate if you can't clearly see what's in it for you. This is not funny or as weird as it sounds. Imagine you are going on a ten-thousand-mile journey by car. Do you think that in those long hours of driving? This repetitive action can become boring if you only look as far as the next stop. You need to keep reminding yourself of the bigger picture to keep your energy going. On such a day, your destination may be the last thing on your mind.

So, it is eminently possible for you to lose sight of the bigger picture in your everyday hurly-burly. You must guard against it, or you won't see the point of being disciplined and working hard. This is what separates the greatest achievers from the run-of-the-mill—they never lose sight of the bigger picture. This ability to never lose sight of your ultimate objective is borne out of immense self-discipline.

Envision the rewards and benefits you can get once you achieve your goals. Nothing compares to the satisfaction when you get things done the way you planned it. Imagine your future self and visualize your goals. Use them as your motivation. Many achievers do a technique that you should practice. Remind yourself how rewarding it feels and how much enjoyment you got from the journey you took to complete the task.

Visualizing your rewards is an excellent technique of ensuring that you never lose focus no matter how many ups and downs you face on the way. Always remember that at the end of it all, the rewards and glory will compensate for all the sacrifices you made along the way.

Practicing self-control and building self-discipline are necessary if you want to be the master of your destiny. Keep your eyes on the long-term benefits rather than the short-term suffering. This will encourage you to work on your self-discipline to improve your overall health and happiness.

The Ten-Second Rule

Before deciding, stop for ten seconds and ask yourself whether the decision is worthwhile. Is the decision needed? Does it bring fulfillment to your life that you haven't already achieved with what you currently possess? Can the decision be foregone?

The ten-second rue will free you from making an unnecessary decision. It also goes ahead to eliminate spontaneity.

Chapter 5:
Become Emotionally Tough

Emotional intelligence is paramount to living a happy, healthy life. It may seem like some people are born with confidence or that some people are predisposed to a high level of emotional intelligence, and depending on the environment in which someone grew up, their background, and life experiences, emotional intelligence may come easier to some people than it does to others. Some people need to work much harder than others to get and maintain a healthy level of emotional intelligence. Luckily, there are ways to improve your emotional intelligence, and all it takes is a little practice and some self-awareness. Emotional intelligence can be improved in many ways, but here are seven methods that you should make a habit of practicing.

Believe Your Intuition
Intuition is that little gut feeling you have or that nagging in the back of your mind when you are trying to decide or decide whether to trust a situation. Our gut feelings or intuition are often based on past experiences in similar situations. Your gut is communicating something to you for a given reason, and often, it tends to be correct. While some people dismiss this feeling, intuitive people listen to what their mind

is trying to tell them. If you have ever had to decide and were leaning heavily toward one outcome or if you've ever been in a situation where your stomach was upset and you felt nervous, that was your intuition trying to tell you something. Some individuals have done something that proved to be beneficial in the end yet couldn't explain why they acted the way they did at the time. Perhaps someone impulsively decided to take a different route to work but couldn't decide what made them decide to take an outer road instead of the highway, only to find out later that they made the right decision because there was a major accident on their usual route to work. Not only did the intuitive person avoid sitting in traffic, but he or she may also have prevented themselves from being involved in a serious or fatal accident. Unexplained decisions or events such as these are your intuition at work.

Intuition is a sign of emotional intelligence. You can improve your intuition by taking the time to spend alone, concentrating on your thoughts, journaling, and paying attention to what your mind is trying to tell you. The mind is a powerful thing, if only we let it work to its full capacity. The more you pay attention to your thoughts, the stronger your intuition will become.

Set Boundaries

Any relationship, whether it's a romantic relationship, a relationship between co-workers, a friendship, or a family relationship, should have healthy boundaries. Emotionally intelligent people recognize their own feelings and can determine if someone else's inappropriate words or actions are causing them to feel uncomfortable. An emotionally intelligent people know what they are willing to put up with and what behaviors are intolerable. Emotionally intelligent people are direct and will tell someone if their language or behavior is making them uncomfortable because they can recognize their own feelings and are in tune with why they feel the way they do. Emotionally intelligent people are also able to set boundaries. They can be assertive because they do not allow themselves to feel guilty for feeling a certain way.

Emotionally intelligent people know what their values are and will not compromise these values. If someone does something to go against what the emotionally intelligent person believes, there will be consequences in place for the behavior. For example, if a friend continues to cancel plans or does not show up when the plans are made, the emotionally intelligent person would recognize that the friend has crossed a boundary, and he or she must decide if the consequence they wish to bestow upon the offending friend is to end the friendship. If someone continues to treat someone else badly but the recipient of the bad behavior continues to allow it to happen, the offender is receiving no consequences and will, therefore, continue to upset the other person with their undesirable behavior. The offender is taking advantage of the other person, who is unwilling or has not chosen to set boundaries. An emotionally intelligent person will let the other person know that his or her behavior is not acceptable. Quite possibly, the offender may not have even known their actions were upsetting to the other person. If the upsetting actions continue, then the offender clearly does not respect the other person's boundaries, and consequences should be enforced, whether that means ending the friendship or keeping the other person at a distance. Emotionally intelligent people have no problem setting boundaries and enforcing these boundaries because they have the self-confidence to know that they are worth receiving fair treatment.

Practice Good Communication

Emotionally intelligent people have excellent communication skills because they know what they want, have set their boundaries, and do not waste time mincing words or saying things that can be construed in a way other than they intended. They also practice good communication skills by listening when speaking to someone.

When conversing with someone, emotionally intelligent people listen to what the other person is saying. They make eye contact and don't become distracted by their phone or other people around them. They listen to hear what is being said; they don't just listen to see how they can respond with their own story. People like to feel appreciated, and anyone who is taking the time to talk to you does not want to be outdone by your story or made to feel like you couldn't wait for their story to end so you could share your own story.

Mental Toughness and True Grit

The emotionally intelligent person also thinks before he or she speaks. If you have only listened to someone else talk so that you could have your own turn, you have not allowed yourself the time to process what they are saying and respond appropriately. The emotionally intelligent person does not just blurt out the first thing that comes to mind; he or she reflects on what the speaker said and respond appropriately.

Another important aspect of good communication is body language. Emotionally intelligent people are in tune not only with themselves but with those around them. Making eye contact, smiling, and keeping your body turned toward the speaker are all signs of good communication skills. Folding your arms, shuffling impatiently back and forth, turning your body away from the speaker, and constantly checking your phone are sure signs that you are not paying attention to what the speaker is saying. Such behavior is rude and does not lend itself to good communication because you are not devoting your full attention to the speaker, which may cause you to miss some key points.

Just as in-person communication skills are vital to a good conversation, an emotionally intelligent person knows that written communication is just as important. Double-check text messages and emails to make sure they say exactly what you intend to say. Remember, mentally tough and emotionally intelligent people will be direct with their words so that the intended meaning of their message cannot be misconstrued. Check for typos or words that have been corrected to mean something else. Read the text message or email out loud to yourself if you are unsure of how it sounds. Taking a few extra seconds to double-check your work is worth the embarrassment of inadvertently sending the wrong message.

Overcome Obstacles in Life

Emotionally intelligent people can overcome obstacles in their lives. They view obstacles as a challenge and often have a game plan and a backup plan in case their original plan does not work. The first step to overcoming an obstacle is to break the process down into smaller, more manageable chunks. It is impossible to write an entire novel in a day, so maybe the emotionally intelligent person will make it his or her goal to write one chapter a week. Likewise, an emotionally intelligent person who has just lost his or her job might make it a goal to apply to three jobs per day, taking the time to perfect his or her cover letter and tailor his or her résumé to each of these jobs. An emotionally intelligent person will then chart his or her progress and reflect on his or her journey. Perhaps he or she will note on a calendar what jobs he or she applied for on what day, or maybe he or she will reflect on how to manage his or her time more wisely to write two chapters of the novel in a week instead of only one chapter.

In addition to setting small goals, an emotionally intelligent person is not afraid to ask for guidance and input or a listening ear at the very least. An emotionally intelligent person embraces challenges and obstacles and welcomes opinions from other sources. He or she knows it sometimes pays to get other perspectives on a situation. He or she knows someone else could bring a new outlook that he or she hadn't thought of. A true emotionally intelligent person welcomes other perspectives while someone who is only acting tough wants to do things his or her own way all the time.

One quick way to overcome an obstacle or get a new perspective is simply to take a break. Go outside. Get some fresh air. Take the dog for a walk. Giving your mind a break and a chance to think about something else will give you a fresh look when you go back to said obstacle. Upon your return, you can evaluate the obstacle. Is this as difficult as it once seemed? A change of scenery could very well change your entire approach.

Maintain A Schedule

An emotionally intelligent person knows there is a benefit to maintain a daily routine. While in our younger days we might have balked at the idea of getting up early and living by a set schedule, an emotionally intelligent person knows a schedule is vital to reducing stress. Imagine if you woke up late every day with no plan for the day. It might sound fun at first, but the truth is, most people would become depressed, sitting around all day with nothing to do; or on the opposite end of the spectrum, they would become stressed out by the number of tasks they need to complete without any rhyme or reason of when these tasks needed to be completed.

If you make a list of all the things you need to accomplish for the day, then cross them off individually when you complete each task. You will be amazed at the sense of accomplishment you feel. Seeing your progress as you make your way down the list not only makes you feel productive, but it is productive. Moving from one task to the next gives you an end goal in sight, and you can see the award of free time, the proverbial light shining at the end of the tunnel.

Not only does this routine give you a feeling of accomplishment, but it helps you eliminate wasted time, much of which is most likely spent making nonessential decisions. For example, if you get into the habit of going to the gym first thing in the morning, you won't have to spend the rest of your day trying to decide when and if you should go; you will already be done for the day.

A mentally strong person thrives on the daily routine because it provides a sense of accomplishment, which also boosts confidence and self-esteem. He or she can track the progress made each day, which in turn motivates the mentally strong person to persevere.

Eliminate Fear of Rejection

Rejection or even the fear of rejection can be very painful, but emotionally intelligent people know that sometimes rejection is just a part of life. They view rejections as one more opportunity for self-improvement and a chance to grow. By practicing a few techniques and improving self-esteem, you can eliminate the fear of rejection. The

Mental Toughness and True Grit

first step to eliminate this fear is to stop assuming you will be rejected in the first place. When people assume, they will be rejected, they subconsciously display behaviors that ultimately get them rejected. The fear of rejection ultimately becomes a reality.

Another way to eliminate the fear of rejection is to picture yourself succeeding. The mind is a powerful thing, and if you think positively, not allowing yourself to picture or see yourself in a rejected state, you can overcome this fear.

A final solution to overcoming the fear of rejection is to give yourself options so that if one thing doesn't work out, you will have other possibilities. Rejection from one job interview does not feel as defeating if you have already lined up other interviews or, at the very least, if you have applied at other places of employment. In today's economy, if you are applying for a job, odds are the company is receiving hundreds, possibly thousands, of applications to fill only one position. It goes without saying that the company will not be able to hire every single person. By applying for several jobs at once or even branching out to consider a different yet similar line of work, you are opening more possibilities for yourself and reducing your fear of rejection.

Emotionally healthy people can keep their minds open to new possibilities and different opportunities even if the new situation is out of their comfort zone. Emotionally healthy people step out of their comfort zone, accept new challenges, and give themselves plenty of options so they do not have to feel rejected by just one person or opportunity.

Reduce Anxiety

An emotionally intelligent person understands that feeling anxious is not beneficial. It is normal to be nervous before a test, a job interview, or a huge presentation. However, when the panicky feelings, upset stomach, rapid heartbeat, and sweaty palms become an everyday occurrence, anxiety is taking its toll on your body and preventing you from achieving your goals. If you let it go on too long, anxiety can snowball and negatively affect your life.

Part of being an emotionally intelligent person is recognizing your feelings and identifying what is causing them. Realizing that you are feeling anxious is the first step. Once you can accept the fact that you are feeling anxious and that it's okay to feel this way, you can identify the source of the anxiety. Begin by asking yourself whether your fears are real. Is the situation or scenario you are imagining likely to happen? Worst-case scenario, if it does happen, will it really matter tomorrow, next week, next month, etc.?

One way to eliminate anxiety is to focus your attention somewhere else. Take a break from what is bothering you and cross a few tasks off that to-do list you made earlier. By accomplishing a goal, you already set for yourself, you will experience a sense of accomplishment

Mental Toughness and True Grit

and improved self-esteem, which are key factors in emotional intelligence.

Chapter 6:
The 40 Percent Rule

The Principle

"He [the Navy SEAL] would say that when your mind is telling you you're done, you're really only 40 percent done. And he had a motto: 'If it doesn't suck, we don't do it'" (Jesse Itzler).

Imagine you're working out at the gym. You're pushing yourself to the very edge of what your body is capable of. After this intense workout, you're exhausted. You just feel like saying, "I just can't do anymore. That's it. I'm spent."

Well, Navy SEALs have a name for that point you reach where you think you're done and where you feel like you can't do anymore.

Do you know what they call it?

They call it the point at which you are 40 percent done.

Also known as "the 40 percent rule," it means you've still got 60 percent left in the tank. You're far from done. Heck, you're not even halfway! If you really wanted, if you rolled up your sleeves, gritted your

Mental Toughness and True Grit

teeth together, and clawed your way onward, you could do another 60 percent.

Jesse Itzler, the co-founder of Marquis Jet, once did a 100-mile race as a relay. While doing that race, he met someone who wasn't doing it as a relay but was doing the *entire* 100 miles alone. As you might've guessed, that someone was a Navy SEAL—David Goggin's, to be exact.

Deciding that he could do with a little of the SEAL's insane mental stamina and ability to put mind over matter, Itzler invited the SEAL to live with him and his family for a month.

The SEAL agreed on one condition: Itzler would do everything he told him to do. (In other words, no "I don't feel like doing that today" nonsense.)

Apparently, Itzler's experience with the SEAL was life-changing because he wrote a book about it, *Living with a SEAL*.

Anyhow, Itzler describes his first day living with a Navy SEAL in an interview with *Big Think*:

The first day that SEAL came to live with me, he asked me to do something. He said, "How many pull-ups can you do?"

I did about eight.

And he said, "All right, take thirty seconds and do it again." So, thirty seconds later, I got up on the bar, and I did six, struggling. And he said, "All right, one more time." We waited for thirty seconds. I barely got three or four, and I was done. I mean I couldn't move my arms. And he said, "All right. We won't move until you perform one hundred more." I thought, well we're going to be here for quite a long time because there's no way that I could do one hundred. But I ended up doing it one at a time. And he showed me, proved to me right there that there was so much more. We're all capable of so much more than we think we are, and it was just a great lesson.

There's a saying—well, not so much a saying as an unspoken rule—that Navy SEALs have. It says, "Capability exceeds belief."

What does that mean?

We all have beliefs about what we are capable of. I personally remember an aunt that used to tell me when I did my school cross-country, "I get tired just watching you." Though, if she *really* wanted, she could run that very same race. Similarly, you might think that there's no way you could do a marathon. However, you almost certainly could.

In other words, *capability exceeds belief*. What you can do exceeds that which your mind thinks you could do—just as the 40 percent rule stipulates.

Mental Toughness and True Grit

Don't believe it? Think it's all just a load of motivational phooey? Well, hold on a second, because science backs it up.

A 2008 study found that participants given a placebo caffeine pill were able to lift significantly heavier weights than participants who were given the caffeine.

What this shows is that the Navy SEALs are right. Mental capacity covers 90 percent while physical fitness covers 10 percent. It's not those who have the biggest biceps that matter but those that have the most grit.

But where does all this extra strength—60 percent extra, to be precise—come from, you ask?

It doesn't come from the body. It doesn't even come from the mind. It comes from sheer will.

But wait, where does one's will come from?

Well, remember *Navy SEAL principle #2*? (Hint: "He who has a *way* to live can bear almost any *how*.")

Your Will Comes from Your Mission—Your Why

Once you have established a definite mission for which you have a burning desire to achieve, mental toughness becomes not so tough. The will to pursue your mission and succeed becomes your powerful driving force.

And of course, there are also the other keys to mental toughness like mastering your self-talk and setting bite-sized goals.

Nonetheless, when it comes to Navy SEALs, the only trait that matters are their ability to push past their own mind and to endure pain without quitting.

The Actionable Takeaway

So next time you're in pain and want nothing more than to quit, remind yourself of the 40 percent rule. Know that if your *why* is strong enough, you'll be able to push yourself that extra 60 percent even when your mind and body are screaming for you not to.

Chapter 7:
Positive Thinking

Everything happens for a reason, and many things can change your life. They can knock you down, or they can lift you up. However, at the end of the day, it all depends on you. It's all in your mind. You, your neighbor, your workmates and your friends all experience the same thing; but what makes it different is how you accept, react to, and view the circumstance.

Every human experience has two dimensions, just like a coin with two sides. It has both a negative component and a positive one, and one weighs heavier than the other, each one bearing different results. When you flip a coin and hold it in your hand, you only see one side, but it doesn't mean that you only have one option. There is another side that exists, and it is up to you to flip it around to train yourself to become a positive thinker.

For example, if you did not get accepted during your job interview, there are two things that you can do. You can give up the job hunt and tell yourself that you are a failure. You can stop hoping that you will be successful in your career, and you can stay right where you are.

Stephen Mark

Or you can exit the interview room, hold your head high, and tell yourself that the job isn't right for you; you will get something better. With this, you went on to look for another job, hoping that you succeed in your endeavor. If you choose the first, you automatically lose the chance for success. It is depriving yourself of the opportunity to be happy. The opposite is true for the second option. Choosing the second option means taking steps to bring you closer toward your goal.

When you have been going through something negative for a long period, such as a divorce or "hopeless" job hunt, you've surely heard people telling you that there is a light at the end of the tunnel. This cliché statement is true in that the bad will not last forever and that you need to have hope.

Believing that a positive thing would come out of something negative is not easy. It may sound like a miraculous event, and people have the tendency to be skeptic about it. How can a bad thing yield a good thing? The thing is what you are going through is not negative. The negativity of it all is just a product of your mind. It will only become negative once you let yourself believe that it is.

Though it is also true that optimism is not just something that can be achieved overnight, it is something that you can achieve with time and practice. You may have been thinking that optimism is just a matter of the mind. Well, there's some truth to it but not entirely. Optimism is also something that you do and say. It can be developed with the

Mental Toughness and True Grit

words you choose to use and the thoughts you choose to let enter your mind.

Chapter 8:
Long-Term Self-Discipline Habits

Define Your Goals

If it all still sounds a little too theoretical, this section will give you step-by-step guides for how to apply the tips of attaining maximum self-discipline in your everyday life.

It'll help you start to develop a willpower plan and give you the tools needed to put that plan into action.

Figure Out What You Want

Sometimes, people get so used to underperforming and playing it safe that they don't even know what their goal is.

They never think about what they truly want because they know, whatever it is, it'll require a lot of work to get, and they're just not up for trying. So, first, put aside the fear of hard work, the fear of failure, and all your "I can't," and just think about what you want for your future.

I don't mean what you want to eat for lunch or what show you'll binge watch on Netflix this weekend. We're talking about the big picture here. What is your ideal future? The first step in acquiring self-discipline is having something to be disciplined for. Hard work is much easier when there's a reason you're doing it.

Really think about it. Take some serious "you time" and come up with a goal for every part of your life—social, romantic, personal, career, and any other significant aspect of your being.

SMART

If you've ever been to a personal trainer to set physical goals or participated in a business course about corporate goal setting, you've most likely encountered the SMART system.

It exists in such wildly different realms as physical fitness and business growth because it really works across most disciplines. Growth can happen in all aspects of life, and it's nice to know there's one tried and true goal setting system you can use for all of them.

So, what is it? *SMART stands for specific, measurable, attainable, realistic, and time bound.*

Specific means you should avoid making vague claims. "I want to lose weight" could be a goal and it's a good start, but it's not exactly painting a picture. There are still questions that need to be answered. Let's take this jumping off point and make it a little more understandable.

The next letter, *M*, for *measurable*, will help with that. A measurable goal has a number attached to it. It answers, "How much?" and "By when?" It helps make your goal more concrete and more understandable. Let's say you want to lose fifty pounds. Now your vague, abstract goal of wanting to "lose weight" is coming into focus.

Measurable is also tied to the last letter in the SMART system, *T* for *time bound*. Attaching a time frame to your goal is another important component of goal setting. It not only makes your goal more specific and measurable but also informs the last two components of SMART.

The next two letters, *A* for *attainable* and *R* for *reasonable*, revolve around whether a person can achieve something and whether you as an individual will meet that target.

Is going to the moon technically achievable? If you don't listen to the conspiracy theorists, then yes, it's totally achievable. Is it reasonable to think that you will become an astronaut? If you aren't one already then, no offense, but probably not. The difference between a thing being possible and a thing being possible *for you* is staggering when you think about it in astronaut terms. Sometimes, what is a walk in the park for someone can be a trip to the moon for another.

Choose your goals according to what is possible in the real world and what is possible for you. Is losing fifty pounds possible? Sure. Possible for you? Maybe.

Mental Toughness and True Grit

This is where you can come back to the T in your goal and tweak it to reflect the possibilities. If you've decided you want to lose fifty pounds, then start to craft a timeline. Will you be able to do it in three weeks? Not. Three months? Probably not. A loss like that will most likely take about six months to a year, depending on your level of commitment.

So again, you go back to the R in your goal and tweak it to reflect your abilities. How many times a week can you get to the gym? Are you a regular healthy eater? Lay out a reasonable plan that will help you reach your goal within your desired time frame.

Do you see how all the letters play off each other? Putting it all together, let's say you want to lose fifty pounds in a year. This goal is reasonable for any given human being and reasonable for you as an individual because you've changed your eating habits and have vowed to go to the gym three to four times a week.

There's your goal! I plan to lose fifty pounds by this time next year by continuing to eat healthy and working out three to four times per week.

It's specific, it's measurable, it has a deadline attached to it, and it's both possible and reasonable for you as an individual.

You can apply the same practice to any goal. Say you want to save enough money for an all-inclusive trip to Cuba by next winter. Is it measurable? You know how much you must save by what date, so yes. Is it attainable? Someone out there could do that, so yes. Is it reasonable? That's where the self-reflection comes in. You'll have to look at your income, spending habits, and debts to know for sure whether you can potentially save that much money by that time. Then you make it specific by implementing a plan.

"I want to save [insert amount] by this date by implementing these money-saving tactics."

Bam! Another SMART goal.

Break It Down

Large goals are scary and, let's face it, kind of easy to give up on. The idea of bringing the bigger picture to life may seem so huge and so far, away that it doesn't even seem possible.

You tell yourself that bailing out on impossible goals is fine, smart even! And suddenly, you've thrown in the towel before you even began. But *very little in life is impossible*. Most things just come down to goal setting and hard work. If you've followed the SMART goals steps and you've got yourself a sweet, manageable, attainable goal, start breaking that goal down into smaller steps.

Going with the above example, if you want to lose fifty pounds by this time next year, where do you start? Probably with losing the first pound, right?

Mental Toughness and True Grit

In the fitness community, there exists a saying that you don't lose X number of pounds—you lose one-pound X amount of times. A huge number like fifty pounds can be too intimidating to get you to even move your butt, but one pound. One is easy. So, figure out what losing that one-pound entails. Focus on that until it happens, and then do it forty-nine more times.

That logic bleeds into every other goal you could possibly have too. You must start with the smallest step forward you can make, then just keep continuing to the next. Everything is less overwhelming when broken down into smaller parts.

Start Practicing

There's a lot of talk in this book about self-discipline being a skill that you can practice and master, but if you need some willpower in the first place to gain greater willpower, you can feel stuck at square one.

It's a bit like that saying, "You have to spend money to make money," but what if you don't have any dough, to begin with? *How do you use something you don't have?*

Start Small

First, recognize that on a scale of 0 to 100, your willpower is probably not an irremediable zero.

You may say you completely lack self-discipline so that you'll have an excuse when you go wild on a Sunday night or max out your credit card buying tacos. However, if you think about it, you'll find that you didn't do any of that because you couldn't stop yourself; you just did it because you felt like it!

That's where you can start exercising some willpower. Feel like you want to do something outrageous that is probably going to be bad for you in the long run? Then, don't do it. Start by not having that last shot at the bar that will almost certainly overdraw your bank account and make it so you can't get out of bed the next day.

It's not a huge sacrifice to not have an extra shot; it's just a small flex of your willpower. Pass by the soda machine at lunch. Don't buy something completely unnecessary. Give up one tiny thing per day you would normally indulge in.

You'll begin to build your confidence in your ability to give things up. You'll start to realize that giving up one or two little indulgences here and there isn't the end of the world. It may not even be difficult. Your old excuse of "I have no willpower" goes completely out the window when you start to do these little flexes.

When you can no longer even convince yourself that you're powerless against your whims, you can start to build up your willpower. All it takes is giving up one thing per day. Not a huge price to pay to increase your self-discipline, is it?

Get Organized

Mental Toughness and True Grit

Practicing willpower can be as simple as getting a to-do list down on paper. I think everyone can relate to going to bed with a full to-do list, convincing yourself you'll get it all done tomorrow, just to make the same promise again the next night.

For some reason, we all tend to believe "tomorrow us" will be much more productive than "today us." Accept that they won't be, and you'll be in a much better mindset to start practicing your willpower today.

You don't have to complete your full to-do list. After all, if you lack willpower, you might have a list a mile long. There are a few strategies people employ when trying to finish a list. Some people like to start with the tasks they want to do the least (the famous "frog to eat" of Brian Tracy). That way, by the time you've done them, the worst is already over, and the rest of the list gets easier and easier. You could also pick one urgent thing and two smaller, less urgent to get done each day. It's not overwhelming, but you will still feel accomplished.

However, you decide to go ahead, the important thing is that you get organized. To-do lists, diaries, journals, household chalkboards, a fridge full of Post-it notes, a trained parrot that recites the things you still need to do, whatever works for you, get an organization system happening.

Create a system for yourself and get that stuff done!

Maintain A Daily Plan

Keep an organized, daily task list. Mapping out the tasks that need to be done daily will give you a better handle on time management. It will also do wonders to improve your self-discipline. How? As you work through each task, checking off one after the other, you will feel energized and pumped to keep going. It's incredibly motivating when you see how much you are accomplishing as your task list slowly begins to shrink. Organized lists are great visual tools to measure daily productivity.

Have Role Models for Inspiration

People admire each other for different reasons. When you admire someone, you put them up on a pedestal; you look up to them like a hero. When one speaks of heroism, it's almost always related to bravery. A hero, from a personal standpoint, is anyone you admire or idolize—not just for bravery but for qualities and achievements. If you want to build self-discipline, it helps to emulate someone you admire.

Who Is Your Hero?

You can choose anyone to emulate. This person could be a family member, a friend, your superior at work, or a known personality. In this context, however, you need to find a hero who's going to be the epitome of self-discipline.

Step 1: Write down a list of individuals you always admire. As already mentioned, this can be anyone: a family member, a friend, a workmate, or a celebrity.

Mental Toughness and True Grit

Step 2: Observe them closely. If you have already been observing them, you must now look even closer so that you can assess your "hero."

Step 3: Choose your top three people. It's best to cut your list down so that you can concentrate on just a few people. They should be people who truly impress you because of their work ethic, character, and personality. You admire them, and their brand of self-discipline is something you know you want for yourself.

Step 4: Study their path to success. How did they become successful? How did they exercise self-discipline in their lives? What are some of the things that they do differently from you?

Step 5: Be your own person. Inspiration eventually wears off. While there are clear benefits you can enjoy from following someone else's footsteps, you still need to be your own individual. If you are too focused on copying, you might lose yourself in the process. Therefore, as soon as you get the rhythm, it is important that you go off-course and journey on your own.

If you want to be more disciplined but do not know how to do so, you can begin by copying someone. You can find someone who projects the type of self-discipline that you want to have in your life, and you can model your actions on them. Maybe you remember yourself as a child when you used to idolize your parents and copied how they did things. Once you pick your hero, you need to study what they do, learn what they say, and basically, try to get inside their head so you can emulate them well.

In the world of self-discipline, a hero doesn't really have to be someone famous. If you think that your workmate is the kind of person you would like to be, then you can emulate them. If you want to make it more personal, you can approach this person and say, "I admire how self-disciplined you are. Can you tell me how you work on being so self-controlled?" Most of the time, this person is going to feel flattered by your admiration and may be willing to mentor you. Whether you get personal coaching directly or simply observe from a distance, remember that emulating people is a good way to master a skill—in this case, self-discipline.

Of course, you cannot expect that it ends with simply imitating someone. The whole business of building self-discipline by emulating someone only begins with you copying your hero. If you are certain about living the same success they enjoy, however, you must become a hero yourself.

How to Become A Hero of Self-Discipline?

After determining who your hero is going to be, it is time to work on being like him or her. Why should you be content with looking up to someone when you can build yourself with the right qualities so that someone else might emulate you as well?

Mental Toughness and True Grit

Naturally, it is easier said than done. Your personal hero has gotten your attention because he or she exemplifies qualities you want to have for yourself, but how can you become a hero too?

- Master perseverance. Your journey toward your goal is not going to be easy. As a matter of fact, it will be long, hard, and full of obstacles. Your capacity to endure will depend on your discipline to see things through to the end. Your hero is a model of self-discipline because he or she persevered and pushed through the obstacles, saying, "Yes, I can," even when being discouraged to push on.

- always Embrace patience. People have varying degrees of tolerance, but most of the time, people have a limit. When things become hard or drag on, your capacity for tolerance is tested. Self-discipline gives you the power to embrace patience even when you think that you have already reached your limit. When you think you have already had enough, patience tells you that you have more to give.

- Always be in control. You oversee your life, and you must be in control of everything that happens to you. A person without control is overcome by a lot of things, and they become mere subjects. Do you desire such a thing for your life? Your heroes did not become heroes because they went along with the tide. They did not become heroes because they lost control of themselves.

As a matter of fact, they were always in charge. A person who has self-discipline is in command of their own thoughts, actions, decisions, and emotions.

- Never lose your drive. People do things for different reasons. This reason is referred to as motivation or drive. Not all people have the drive to make things happen, but those who do are the ones who are truly accomplished in life. They operate with the right drive, and they are achievers. It's like they consumed large quantities of an energy drink and have a lot of fire in them. A person with self-discipline will never lose the drive to push forward. They are always full of energy to make things happen.

- Learn to commit. It's easy for one to say they will do something—what's hard is to make the move to act on it. Then once you're on track, it's even harder to stay on it and commit. Commitment demands so much from people, but when you have self-discipline, you develop the capacity to fulfill a promise no matter its extent. Saying that you will get something done is easier, but it's much harder to keep that promise when conditions are convincing you to go another way.

- Always choose good over evil. Whenever you are faced with a choice, always choose good over evil because you know that it is for the good of more people. It takes a lot of discipline to choose the right thing, but the power you develop to battle against evil is what will make you a hero.

- No one is demanding that you become a superhero. You are not being asked to sacrifice your life for someone else, but heroes come in different packages. Like your personal heroes for self-discipline, you must try to be a good model of self-control so that you can be a unique version of a hero throughout your life.

Self-Discipline Is Not A One-Time Thing

If you truly want to be successful just like your role models, you to have to make self-discipline a part of who you are. It is not just a trait you bring out once or twice. If you want positive changes in your life, self-discipline must be ingrained in you—second nature.

Stay Focused and Track Progress

When did you the last concentrate and focus hard on a task until you saw it all the way through? Or when was the last time you set a goal for yourself that you were determined to reach no matter what challenges were thrown your way? Finish what you start. See things through. It's what productive and successful people do every single day.

Nothing gives your self-discipline a bigger boost than to see how far you have progressed on a task. Make it a habit at work to consistently track your assigned tasks. Indicate what has already been done and what is yet to be finished. Hence, when you feel your discipline dwindling, taking a quick look at your progress chart will be the nudge you need to keep going.

Setting Priorities

People have different needs, wants, and desires. What sets the successful people apart is that they have their priorities in order. They direct their focus and attention toward nurturing those priorities until they come to fruition.

Setting the right priorities is crucial. It can be easy to get overwhelmed by all the tasks you need to get done. When you're overwhelmed, you'll often end up frustrated, stressed, and burned out. It becomes hard even to think straight. Any productive momentum you may have had will quickly diminish. Clear and specific priorities will give you better clarity about what needs to be addressed first and, ideally, can help you determine which tasks will be the most beneficial to you.

Overcome Negativity

Negative thought patterns are usually strong and may have devastating impacts on all spheres of our lives. By thinking negatively, we are creating a crisis within ourselves that ultimately leads to failure. However, with practice, every person who is ready and willing can break free of negative thinking once and for all. Being drawn into a negative thinking pattern is the same as building a prison within your own mind. It will hold you captive and render you useless.

Humankind has struggled with negative thoughts and has come up with different ways in which they can break out of the situation. Unfortunately, some of them have adopted inappropriate ways to drown their sorrows through drugs. This, however, works temporarily and will never be a long-term solution. Once the drugs' effects are long gone, you will still find yourself stuck in the same situation you are in before the intake of drugs.

Overcoming negativity and the self-hating perceptions that makes you a miserable person can be overcome through the cultivation of inner happiness and peace. The following are some of the proven ways in which you can get out of negativity.

Recognizing Negative Thought Patterns

Negative thought patterns refer to unproductive and repetitive thoughts. These thoughts do not serve any purpose, and they cause negative emotions. The moment you learn how to recognize and single out these thought patterns the moment they occur, you will have good control on how you should react. Some of the common negative thinking patterns include the following:

1. Anxious Thoughts and Worries

By imagining or even expecting that bad things will occur or nothing substantial will ever happen to you, your health will start deteriorating. The relationships that you have with your friends, co-workers, and family will go downhill, and ultimately, your career could also be ruined.

The interesting part regarding this is that even though the events have not yet happened, they have already taken a negative effect on your health. At times, you may focus on the emptiness of your life and start getting stressed about the welfare of your children, the financial future, or even your partner leaving you for someone else.

2. Criticism and Self-Beating

With this negative pattern, you find that you are harsh and overly critical of yourself. You focus on your weaknesses and the perceived flaws. People with this negative pattern can also affect others. Criticism and self-beating often result in lack of confidence and low self-esteem. To compensate for the low self-esteem, they look for recognitions, achievements, and status while some may isolate themselves, allowing only minimal contact with other people.

3. Regret and Guilt

If you ruminate on mistakes made in the past, you can easily find yourself in regret and guilt. Some bad decisions that you made in the past can arouse feelings of worthlessness and guilt. Although there is nothing wrong with reflecting on past events and experiences, the problem comes when you isolate an event in the past and dwell on it.

4. Detaching Yourself from Negative Thinking

People at times feel hopeless because they are not sure of what to do. In such circumstances, positive thinking becomes difficult. Whenever you feel down, try to spend some time with people you love and ask them for support and a dose of positivity. Talk to them about what you have achieved so far and what you are planning to do next. This will give you a boost of happiness and enthusiasm. Keep your mind focused on the positive thoughts, and always remind yourself of your goal.

5. Becoming the Watcher of Thoughts

You must pay attention to whatever is going through your mind at any given time. By becoming a curious observer of the things that go on within your internal environment, you will become better placed to handle and respond to negative thought patterns.

The mind works like a record that plays old tunes repeatedly. Because of lack of awareness, the record continues playing in line with its momentum. By having deliberate and conscious attention to your thought patterns, you will be able to attain a higher level of awareness.

6. Impartial Witness

Whenever you observe your emotions and thought patterns, you need to be an impartial witness. As an impartial witness, you need to be careful that you are not carried away or involved in emotions and thoughts. Just stay as a watcher. The aim of impartial witness and the watcher of thoughts are basically to enable you to detach yourself from negative thought patterns.

7. Be Mindful of The Moment

According to James Thurber, we should not look back with anger or look forward with fear, but rather, we should look around with awareness. Negative thoughts usually flow from two directions. The first place of dwelling for negative thought patterns is the past. This is where you may find yourself thinking over problems and mistakes that you made in the past.

The second source for negative thought patterns is the future. Because we are uncertain of what will happen in the future, we tend to fear and think negatively about things that may never happen. This gives you stress because at times you may feel that the future has collapsed on you.

To be aware of your environment, use your senses to the fullest. Do not regard the things that you did in the past will likely happen in the future. This will give you the opportunity to focus on the present with undivided attention. Try as much as possible to create awareness of the scents, sounds, and sensations in the air. This focus on the present is necessary to calm you down and overcome negativity.

Choose Positive Thoughts Instead of Negative

After creating inner awareness through the ways discussed above, you should change your thinking so that it becomes constructive rather than destructive. Positive thoughts will help you to deal with your day-to-day challenges effectively. Instead of ruminating over the past, you can use those experiences to adjust your current situations so that you do not make the same mistake.

Worrying will cause anxiety and grief. There are some constructive actions that you can engage in, such as traveling or fixing a leakage around your home. With constructive thinking, you can be assured that even when things are not going well, you can afford to smile.

The more you practice awareness of thinking patterns, the more you will realize that you are slowly redirecting yourself into the path of positivity and growth.

Chapter 9:
5 Secrets to Building Mental Toughness

1. Wake Up Early and Get Out of Bed.

Always wake up twenty minutes earlier. I know, to most of us, sleep is a precious resource that we never have enough of. Health experts recommend six to eight hours per night and that can really be a struggle for many of us with jobs, kids, and chores around the house. With that said, having an extra twenty minutes in the morning can help knock out some of those dreaded chores or, at the very least, help to prevent you from rushing around in the morning, trying to get out the door. This rush will inevitably kick off your day with a stress-filled anxiety attack. Starting your day in this manner can have halo effects on everything else you do that day and can prevent you from living your best life to the fullest potential.

I am not saying that setting your alarm twenty minutes earlier will not be a challenge, especially at first. This is one piece that will take some getting used to, but I promise, you will adapt, and you will thank me later. I think you will find that it will take less time than you think to get your body acclimated and ready to roll on twenty minutes less sleep. If it is a challenge after some days, there is always the option of going to bed twenty minutes earlier.

Now that you have your alarm set twenty minutes earlier, the hard part starts. You must *wake up and get out of bed* when the alarm goes off. You may need to try tricks like placing your alarm clock far away from the bed, so you must get up to go and switch it off. *Remove the snooze*. I promise you'll love it (although maybe not at first).

For me, getting up earlier has had many life-changing benefits. First, I've found that I really enjoy the quietness of my house. There is something very soothing about a dark and quiet house while I have my coffee. Also, it gives me time to do something that maybe I've been putting off. Sometimes, when I'm feeling ambitious, I'll put on a YouTube video of a beginner's twenty-minute yoga routine. I've discovered that it really gets my blood pumping while helping me calm down and relax all at the same time. Finally, as mentioned above, I feel less rushed when I get up a few minutes earlier, which sets the tone for a peaceful, positive, and productive day.

2. Make Your Bed.

Once you wake up, make your bed. I know it seems like a small and trivial task, but I have a feeling it will work wonders for you. It is a task that only requires a few minutes of your time but can help jumpstart your day in ways you have probably never dreamed imaginable. Key benefits include the following:

- Starting your day with productivity. Starting out with something productive will help you maintain that mindset as you face more difficult challenges throughout your day.

- Starting your day with something active. Get up, get moving, and get the blood flowing to activate the awesomeness coming your way today.

- Starting your day by checking something off your list. Completing a task can set off a chain reaction of activities designed at completing more tasks. Start with something small and work your way up to something huge!

- Starting your day with a win. It is always a positive thing when you start out your day with a goal and then you achieve it, no matter how small that goal may be.

In addition to the many benefits making your bed has on the start of your day, it can be beneficial to the end of your day as well. A made bed is considerably more appealing to crawl into after you've just crushed your day. And with any luck, the appealing bed you so diligently made earlier this morning will produce a better night's rest to help you move even closer to your goal's tomorrow.

Already make your bed every day. Spend time reflecting on how it is a positive thing in your life that is helping you achieve your goals. I'd be willing to bet; you've never thought about this daily routine as something that will drive you closer to your dream life.

3. Carry Heavy Shit.

The first body of thought on mental toughness centers on proper physical maintenance of your entire body. You can't run a quality microchip inside a broken machine.

You need to exercise. A study conducted by the Georgia Institute of Technology found that a high-intensity workout that lasted only twenty minutes had the ability to enhance episodic memory in healthy young adults by approximately 10 percent.

Lifting weights has been associated with improving a person's memory as well. However, according to common wisdom, it does not have to be a specific type of exercise; any type of physical activity helps your memory function better.

4. Study First.

Develop a hunger for books. The more inspirational they are, the better—any book that will drive your determination, self-discipline, and willpower. Stock up on books that equip and empower you to realize your dreams. Fill your library with them.

Successful people read a lot; thus, they are in perpetual control of their thoughts, projecting only what they want into their reality. You are currently joining the early phases of learning to be in the driver's seat, to be the one in control of your mind instead of giving it this same power. These early phases are the most crucial. It's when your mind is beginning to relearn, regrow—a rebirth, if you will. To help it along its growth, you need to feed it with the nourishment that comes in the form of inspirational books. Devour regularly and consistently. Build an impressive library of inspirational content at home or on your mobile device that you can readily access.

5. Eat Something You Don't Like.

Mental toughness is about being ready to pass through extremely negative scenarios for you to attain the extremely positive results. Taking this step, you will find yourself in a position to tolerate the challenges that come up when you eat what you dislike. You will get used to them and enjoy their taste with time.

Chapter 10:
The 7 Rules for Success

1. Keep Working Hard

Successful individuals do not spend too much time thinking about their talents and/or their luck in life. They know that hard work and effort are what matter most at the end of the day. A mix of hard work, discipline, determination, drive, and willpower is the winning combination that you need. No amount of talent or luck can substitute for hard work. They push themselves to keep going where so many would rather give up. It's this tenacity that makes all the difference in the world.

Again, like a physical muscle, there is no shortcut to increased self-discipline. You must put in the time, effort, and energy if you want to make it happen. With more discipline, you'll see more positive changes in your life. However, you'll need to make sacrifices and adjustments. There will be difficult challenges ahead, but it'll all be worth it.

The road to self-discipline is going to put you to the test and push you beyond your comfort zone. However, it will also make you a much stronger and better person. There is a reason why we often hear successful individuals attribute their success to hard work and self-discipline.

2. Find Your Drive

What do you intend to acquire from life? It is not enough to say, "I want to be successful," "I want wealth," "I want to be somebody important," or "I want to be a leader." While these general statements are a good start, a more specific vision in mind will help you focus and narrow down the steps you need to work on. Naturally, everyone wants to be successful, and no one will say no to success. However, in what exactly do you want to be successful?

Finding your mission can be difficult when you think you lack the talent. It can be even more difficult when you have low self-esteem and don't believe in yourself at all. Although some seem to be born with natural talents, the rest of us may require more time and effort to discover what we excel in. Some may not even realize that they have the potential to be outstanding until pushed to their limit. Hence, keep in mind that there is always something you can shine in. You just need to discover it. Perhaps, leaving your comfort zone may even be the key to finding it. You will never know unless you try.

Set a goal for yourself. You can always start with a small goal and then build momentum and confidence from there. Write it down. Having clear written goals will make them real and will help you define what needs to be accomplished. Thus, your goals are no longer random thoughts and ideas in your head that are soon forgotten. Write them down, maybe more than once. Bring this list everywhere with you. Look at it each time you need to remind yourself of your goal and why you're doing what you're doing.

3. Be Different

If there is one thing that productive and successful people do, it is that they never shy away from a challenge. In fact, they embrace every challenge and treat it as a personal mission to see how they will overcome it. They ride on the thrill of accomplishments, which motivates them and keeps them going. Challenges, for them, are opportunities for improvement. It can be tempting to stay comfortable and slack off occasionally, but new challenges train your self-discipline to be better.

Start embracing challenges. They will be a part of your story each time you work on accomplishing a new goal.

4. Fail Your Way to Success

Considering a setback as a gift instead of a curse may be the last thing on your mind. However, this method works. If you think about the past challenges and setbacks that you faced that you managed to overcome eventually anyway, instead of looking at the downside, consider the takeaway lessons each setback left you with. Did it make you a much stronger person? Did it turn out to be a blessing in disguise? Did it add something of value to your life in a way you might not otherwise have had the opportunity of experiencing? If you can train yourself to view each setback as a gift instead of a demotivating element, you will do wonders to transform your persistence and levels of self-discipline.

5. Have High Expectations

Staying motivated and persistent is a challenge when you cannot directly see the result. Working endlessly while wondering when you'll see the fruit of your labor is not something everyone can do. This situation highlights why self-discipline is again of the utmost importance. Without it, successful people would not have made it as far as they did. It takes sheer grit, determination, and—you guessed it—self-discipline to stay on track no matter what may come your way. Many of them had to wait, some for several years. They had to keep working toward their goals before it became a reality and all their hard work paid off. It's such type of work ethic that you need to start emulating if you also want to emulate their success.

Successful people have taught themselves how to visualize, how to see themselves at the end of their goals, achieving success with a smile on their face. They visualize the picture so vividly, motivating themselves to do anything to reach their goal. Visualization is a powerful tool that should be made a part of your daily routine. It can be transformative. When you can see and feel a goal so clearly in your mind, clear enough to believe that it is real, focusing on it will fuel your desire to make that vision a reality.

6. Have A Clear Vision and Goal

When you want to achieve something, however big or small, it helps if you visualize the outcome you desire. The plan you have just written for yourself is supposed to be a personal design that will take you from one point to another.

Visualization takes you to your goal even before you physically get there. It is powerful because of the following reasons:

- It activates your subconscious. If you think it, then it will happen. The power of visualization has the power to stimulate your subconscious mind so that you are programmed to achieve your goals.

- It attracts positive energy. Have you heard of the law of attraction? The law of attraction dictates that things that happen in the universe are the result of the power of the mind to manifest outcomes by simply thinking positive thoughts. You attract what you think. Therefore, if you are a stubborn pessimist, then you will only attract bad karma into your life. Positive visualization, on the other hand, will attract positive outcomes.

- It programs your brain accordingly. As already mentioned, self-discipline is first and foremost a mindset. When you succeed at programming your brain through visualization, you become more perceptive to stimuli, making you more capable of achieving your goals.

- It motivates your journey. Every dream you have required fuel. You need a drive that will propel you toward your goal; and in the case of developing the right discipline to be able to achieve your goals, visualization will give you the necessary fuel.

You can do visualization exercises throughout the day. One example is the mental rehearsal, which you can carry out a few times a day. A mental rehearsal allows you to go through an event, however positively you wish for it to go, and assume it as a reality.

Another example of visualization is to use images. Vision boards are very popular in relation to the law of attraction. People who follow the law of attraction are encouraged to create vision boards that make use of images and words of affirmation to represent their dreams and aspirations. Visualization is about putting things out there. It encourages you to expect results before they even happen because such a winning attitude helps you harness an inner power.

7. Stop Making Excuses

A good practice of self-discipline demands that you have accountability. This is twofold: personal responsibility that compels someone to claim ownership of their own actions and indirect responsibility that compels a person to help someone else. Both forms show admirable character because, truth be told, not everyone is going to assume responsibility.

Mental Toughness and True Grit

One most difficult feat you will encounter is sustaining a consistent level of discipline from beginning to end. If things move in a way not planned and you slip, you do not have to make excuses for what you have done or have failed to do. If things are not exactly as you had expected them to be, you do not have to keep complaining about it. Complaints and excuses are for the weak.

When you make yourself accountable, it shows that you have respect for yourself and others. The decisions you make today always have a long-term effect, whether you realize it now. It is this before-the-fact mindset that you maintain that you carry with you wherever you go—and one that you apply to everything. This, of course, comes with a corresponding after-the-fact mindset that will compel you to act according to the results of your previous behavior.

Every action has an equal reaction; being self-disciplined means taking responsibility for all of this—not enjoying the habit of making excuses and complaints. Your journey is not going to be all smooth sailing. You will encounter struggle, and you will burn out at times, so you need to be truly committed.

Chapter 11:
Call to Action

It is possible that you agree with everything that you have read in the book so far. You agree with it yet think that self-discipline is something that you can't get your head around. You know that you need to do something about it. You have heard others say that to you, but you know yourself, and you don't think that you have it in you to be self-disciplined.

Well, you may believe that you are the only person that thinks that way, but that is not true. There are so many who have given up on themselves when it comes to mending their wayward ways. But you know neither you nor anyone else who thinks like that is right. You are simply procrastinators who don't want to deal with the underlying causes of your lack of self-discipline.

Come to think of it—quite many people don't really know what self-discipline all those of you is about, especially who are very young. You can understand as you go along in life, undergoing a myriad of experiences. Of course, there are some who seem to be gifted with the unique ability to exercise the right amount of rectitude and restraint at the right time.

Very early on in life, you have got to understand that the only thing that will ensure that you don't get stuck in mediocrity and grow to realize your potential is that you learn to make the right choices in life, even if these are difficult ones. If, as a child, you showed potential as a tennis player, you would be able to fulfill this dream only if you agreed to forego having fun with your school friends after school and instead head for hours of grueling tennis practice, day after day, year after year.

Difficult or even impossible for someone like you, you are thinking, but there are thousands of kids around the country who do it. They don't come from another planet, but they have something that many others don't—apart from their talent, a keen foresight and the willingness to work hard to capitalize on their potential. Now it is possible that the motivation comes from their parents, teachers, or coaches; but until they can believe in the dream, they will not exercise the required discipline.

It needn't be tennis. It could simply be getting a well-paid job. Great discipline must come from high motivation. There has got to be something in your life, the pursuit of which drives you at a subliminal level. Having a drive or ambition is wired into the human being's genetic makeup. If you dig deep enough, you will surely find it in yourself.

The thing is that the modern times do not require you to hunt for survival like it did in the times of your caveman ancestors. If they had wasted time procrastinating, they would either have gone hungry or been killed and eaten up by a predator. It was "kill or get killed" for them. The objective in those days was simple survival.

So, self-discipline came naturally to them, for it was a matter of life and death for them. You may not have to kill wild animals for your daily survival, but it would be good if you could bring some of the intensity of focus that your ancestors brought to their daily actions in achieving your short-term goals. Over time, you will see that the most difficult of your long-term objectives will have been met.

Some of the greatest religions of the world were born out of the conviction and teachings of certain strong-willed men. They were so gifted in their ability that they were able to galvanize their chief disciples to go forth and spread their word far and wide, and it would be so often that those highly focused and disciplined people would be able to do their master's bidding so well that, within a few centuries, those faiths became world religions.

Faiths like Christianity and Buddhism became world religions on the back of the extraordinary self-discipline shown by monks and nuns through the millennia in setting examples to the world by their austere personal conduct and getting others to join their faith. If you

Mental Toughness and True Grit

have a mission that you believe in, you will go to any length to bring it to fruition.

So, you see where we are coming from here? You really should believe in what you are doing for you to dedicate yourself in a disciplined manner to its fulfillment. If you are someone of weak faith, whether in religion or your expectations from yourself, discipline is not to be expected from you.

If you feel that this is a situation that you are not comfortable with, then you will surely take the required steps to rectify the situation. Being around people who are disciplined and in an environment that is conducive to that kind of thinking helps. Reading about achievers and what they did to become the way they are helps too.

Let your brain's wiring change by the right kind of exposure, and it will carry you to the most incredible destinations in life. The ability to overcome your natural propensity to indulge in impulsive activities requires for you to have self-control. Now, this is something that can be improved with the right kind of effort.

If you are aware of your goals and realize the importance of achieving them, you will be more amenable to exercising self-control. If, for example, you decide to study hard to graduate with good grades to get a good job, you will be aware of the negative consequences of failing.

Studies of the human brain show that the right frontal cortex has a crucial role in how much self-control an individual has. Damage to this part often leads to less self-control and restraint on the part of an individual. So, if certain people don't seem to be very self-disciplined and responsible, this may be the reason why.

That being stated, people with cohesive and happy families who live in a stimulating and conducive environment will find it easier to be self-disciplined, responsible, and with a fair idea about where they are heading in life and what they need to do to get there.

One thing that should give heart to most people who try to discipline themselves but don't seem to be getting where they want to be is the fact that self-discipline does not come about quickly or overnight. You must develop it over time.

According to Einstein, it takes a minimum of ten years of hard work for one to start tuning into the performances of a genius. Along the way, you must be ready to make the sacrifices required. You must be willing to focus only on what needs to be done to achieve your long-term goal rather than doing something that gives you pleasure over the short term.

If becoming a concert pianist was your dream, then daily practice would have to take priority over hanging out with your pals over a beer. It is not easy, especially when the exercise of discipline stretches across long years, with the expected rewards being many years into the future. This is the time when you should be able to display the necessary grit required to stay the course.

The thing about instant gratification is that this is something that the society encourages because it does not know or care about your goals. People are perfectly happy to have you come over for a party or to play bridge. It is you who is responsible for fulfilling your passion.

So, it does not matter that you are not able to make time for your friends and spend all your waking hours working toward the success of your startup. You may find the going tough, and you may face heartbreaks along the way. However, if you are willing to remain steadfast in your commitment to your goal, you will get there. This is what self-discipline does for you. It is an enabler, a miracle worker.

Since you know now that self-discipline is an incredibly powerful tool that can help you achieve your much-cherished goals, you should do everything within your powers to develop it. Here's what might help you with it.

- Our capacity for self-discipline exists for whatever we set our minds on achieving. So, if instead of watching news incessantly and becoming an expert on current affairs, you focused on growing your business—you would be much better served.

- Self-discipline becomes easier with practice. The more you exercise it, the better you become at it. Say you are a pretty decent tennis player but just can't hit a backhand stroke, because, as a child, you had once fallen and broken your arm when trying that stroke. You need to spend more time practicing your weakness.

- If you work with your coach to overcome your long-held fears and try learning that stroke all over again, you may find it tough at first, but if you persist and practice long enough, you will be able to bring it on par with your other strokes.

- If you don't eat well on account of lack of time or any other reason, you will suffer a depletion of willpower, which will make it difficult for you to exercise self-control. So, eat in a manner that leaves you energized enough to perform at optimal or near optimal capacity.

- Just as the body needs enough nutrition, it needs the required quantity of sleep for you to effectively be able to display self-discipline.

- Get into the habit of performing tasks in order of priority and not in order of ease. This will achieve an excellent and well-honed sense of self-discipline in you.

- One last thing is about the fact that exercising self-discipline consistently does extract a toll on your reserves of ego, because you put so much commitment into it. It is okay to take a break sometimes. Indulge in a hobby or give into a weakness occasionally. If you are training to be a boxing champion, occasionally having that ice cream doesn't hurt. Even machines need to be serviced sometimes, and you are only human.

Self-discipline is not just a quality for life but also a quality that will change your life in ways you cannot even imagine until you begin doing it and see it happen right in front of you. You don't have to be disgruntled and unhappy with a mediocre life. You now possess the knowledge and the tools that you need to begin turning your life around.

If you find this book helpful in anyway a review to support my endeavors is much appreciated.

www.ingramcontent.com/pod-product-compliance
Lightning Source LLC
Chambersburg PA
CBHW060552080526
44585CB00013B/536